THE COMPLETE ILLUSTRATED ENCYCLOPEDIA OF THE

LANCASTER
BOMBER

T0150152

THE COMPLETE ILLUSTRATED ENCYCLOPEDIA OF THE
LANCASTER BOMBER

THE HISTORY OF BRITAIN'S GREATEST NIGHT BOMBER OF WORLD WAR II, IN MORE THAN 275 PHOTOGRAPHS

NIGEL CAWTHORNE

southwater

This edition is published by Southwater
an imprint of Anness Publishing Ltd
info@anness.com
www.southwaterbooks.com
www.annesspublishing.com

Anness Publishing has a new picture agency outlet for images for publishing,
promotions or advertising. Please visit our website www.practicalpictures.com
for more information.

A CIP catalogue record for this book is available from the British Library.

Previously published as *Lancaster: WWII Night Bomber and Dambuster*

Produced for Anness Publishing Ltd by Editorial Developments, Edgmond,
    Shropshire, England
Design: Bacroom Design and Advertising
Index: Marie Lorimer Indexing Services
Production Controller: Ben Worley

PUBLISHER'S NOTE
Although the information in this book is believed to be accurate and true at the time of
going to press, neither the author nor the publisher can accept any legal responsibility
or liability for any errors or omissions that may have been made.

Contents

Right: During World War I, this was the way aerial bombing was carried out. The pilot or passenger would lean over the side of the aircraft and drop bombs on the enemy below.

Lancaster Bomber

Aircraft changed the face of war. In the early 20th century some romantics saw the dogfights over the trenches as a return to the hand-to-hand combat of the age of chivalry, as opposed to the wholesale industrialized slaughter that was going on below. But something more terrible was taking place.

In December 1911, during the Italo-Turkish War of 1911–12, an Italian pilot on an observation mission reached over the side of his plane and dropped grenades on the Turks below. It was the first recorded incident of aerial bombardment. During World War I, both German and Allied airmen followed suit. Soon purpose-built bombs were made. Then on 19 January 1915, a German Zeppelin appeared over Norfolk and dropped bombs on Great Yarmouth, Sheringham and King's Lynn, killing 20 and seriously injuring another 40. These towns had no strategic importance. Civilians were being deliberately targeted.

After the war was over, strategists sat down to figure out what could be learned from the conflict. One of them was Basil Liddell Hart, who developed a new theory of mechanized warfare. This was largely ignored in Britain, but in Germany Heinz Guderian used it to develop the Panzer and his own theory of Blitzkrieg.

By 1925, Liddell Hart had moved on. He published a book called *Paris, or the Future of War*. In it, he attacked the Allies' strategy in World War I which, he said, was based on the ideas of the 19th-century Prussian general and military theorist Carl von Clausewitz. Following von Clausewitz's principles, they had sought to destroy the enemy's armed forces in the main theatre of war. This had led to the senseless slaughter in the trenches of the Western Front.

What the Allies should have done, he said, was find the enemy's weakest point and attack him there – like Paris shooting his arrow into Achilles' heel: whence came the title of his book. The enemy's weakest point, Liddell Hart argued, was not their army, but their willingness to fight. With people and industry packed together into cities, modern society was very vulnerable to dislocation, he reasoned. Aircraft dropping bombs or even poison gas into their cities would paralyse any country.

"Imagine for a moment London, Manchester, Birmingham, and half a dozen other great centres simultaneously attacked," he wrote, "the business localities and Fleet Street [then the London home of Britain's national newspapers] wrecked, Whitehall a heap of ruins, the slum districts maddened into the impulse to break loose and maraud, the railways cut, factories destroyed. Would not the general will to resist vanish, and what use would be the still determined fractions of the nation, without organization and central direction?"

In *The British Way in Warfare*, published in 1932, he pointed out that Britain had built its empire by avoiding land wars and relying instead on its sea power. World War I had been an aberration and Britain had learned to its cost what happened when it tried to emulate the great land powers and put a large number of men in the field. He then became a passionate advocate of air power, arguing that bombing alone could bring an enemy to its knees.

Left: The damage shown here is from the Zeppelin bombing of the Great Yarmouth area in England during World War I.

Left: The remains of the Basque market town of Guernica after the German bombing raid in 1937 during the Spanish Civil War. The Luftwaffe's Condor Legion had developed the art of carpet bombing. It was a technique that the Lancasters of Bomber Command would use to great effect during World War II.

Again the Germans learned the lesson. On 27 August 1937, German bombers attacked the Basque market town of Guernica. Although there were military targets in the town – a communications centre and a munitions factory – there is no indication that the German bombers aimed for them. They simply dropped bombs indiscriminately on civilians. A report sent back to Berlin said this carpet bombing had been a "great success". Guernica fell two days later and the victory of the Nationalists – Germany's ally – was complete in 1939. By that time, the Japanese had taken to carpet bombing Chinese cities. It was plain that, in the European war that now seemed inevitable, bombers would play a key role and the British Air Ministry began issuing specifications for heavy bombers – first with two engines, then with four. When war broke out on 1 September 1939, a number were already in full production.

On 1 August 1940, Hitler signed Führer Directive No. 17, ordering the Luftwaffe to smash the RAF as quickly as they could. Germany needed to dominate the skies if it was to succeed in invading Britain. German planes were to take the RAF on in the air and attack their ground facilities and supply centres. They were to bomb aircraft factories and factories producing anti-aircraft guns. They were also to attack the ports that brought in vital supplies – leaving intact the Channel ports that would be needed in the invasion. However, British cities were not to be terror-bombed without the express order of Hitler himself.

Right: Die Wehrmacht *was the official magazine of the German Armed Forces. This particular copy shows a Stuka dive-bomber, dropping a bomb supposedly over England, with the words "Ihre bomben lassen England erzittern", which roughly translated means "your bombs leave England trembling violently".*

Hitler's plan almost succeeded. By mid-August, the RAF's Fighter Command was on its last legs. It had lost 1,000 pilots and the Germans were sending up to 1,500 planes a day to attack its airfields. Then, on the evening of 24 August, a German plane accidentally bombed non-military targets in London. Churchill immediately ordered a retaliatory attack on Berlin. The next night, 81 twin-engined bombers took off for the German capital. Only 29 planes made it. The others got lost on the way; 8 men were killed and 28 wounded. The damage to Berlin was slight, but Hitler had promised the German people that such a thing would never happen. Infuriated, he abandoned the 1 August Directive and ordered the terror-bombing of London.

The German bombing campaign that followed was called the Blitz. It began on 7 September when 330 tons of bombs were dropped on London. The terror-bombing campaign was later extended to Liverpool, Coventry and other cities. Although the population suffered terribly from these attacks, the RAF had a breathing space to recover.

The British Army had withdrawn from continental Europe in May 1940. Bombing was the only way they could take the battle to the enemy. At first, they aimed to attack military targets, but it was soon shown that 'precision' bombing was in fact highly inaccurate, so the idea of saturation bombing was developed. Huge resources were put into building heavy bombers that could pulverize German cities, attempting, as Liddell Hart had advocated, to win the war by destroying the enemy's will to fight.

The plane leading the attack was the Lancaster bomber. It could carry a greater bomb load than any other RAF bomber, flew more sorties and did greater damage. From its first attack on Germany on 10 March 1942 until D-Day on 6 June 1944 it was Britain's key frontline weapon in the war in Europe. Its role continued: it bombed railways and bridges, preventing the Germans from bringing up reinforcements to push the Allies back to the sea. It continued pounding German cities until 19 April 1945 – two weeks before Germany surrendered.

The bombing of cities may not have been the war-winning tactic that Liddell Hart and others had hoped. But without it – and the Lancaster – the war would almost certainly have been lost. During the bleakest years of the war, bombing raids against German cities were vital for British morale. At least the beleaguered island was fighting back, and the Lancasters' most famous action – the Dambusters raid in May 1943 – came at a vital moment, showing the Americans that the British had the will and the means to fight on.

Below: An aerial photograph taken during the evening attack on the V-2 assembly and launching bunker at Wizernes, France. An Avro Lancaster of 103 Squadron is flying over the target area, which is covered by the smoke from high-explosive and incendiary bombs.

Winston Churchill : House of Commons – 18 June 1940

"...*but we must never forget that all the time, night after night, month after month, our bomber squadrons travel far into Germany, find their targets in the darkness by the highest navigational skill, aim their attacks, often under the heaviest fire, often with serious loss, with deliberate careful discrimination, and inflict shattering blows upon the whole of the technical and war-making structure of the Nazi power.* **"**

Chapter One

Dambusters

O n 16 May 1943, the Lancaster bombers of the RAF's 617 Squadron took off on the most famous bombing raid of World War II. The aim was to breach the hydro-electric dams that powered the armaments factories of the Ruhr Valley, and flood Germany's industrial heartland.

Although the newly formed 617 Squadron had been in training for eight weeks, they had only been told of their target at the briefing that evening at 1800 hours. Three hours later, the seven-man crews of the first two waves were driven out to their Lancasters to go through final checks. They ran their engines, then shut them down awaiting the signal to go.

Above: The attack on the Möhne, Eder and Sorpe dams by 617 Squadron on the night of 16/17 May 1943 was named Operation Chastise. Shown here is a practice Upkeep weapon, attached to the bomb bay of Wing Commander Guy Gibson's Avro Type 464 (Provisioning) Lancaster, ED932/G AJ-G, at Manston, Kent, while conducting dropping trials off Reculver in England. The 10,000lb Upkeep rotating mine was held in the modified bomb bay between a pair of side-swing callipers, and rotated via a belt drive to a hydraulic motor mounted in the forward fuselage.

Right: King George VI examining the Möhne dam model with Air Vice Marshal Sir Ralph Cochrane, Wing Commander Gibson and Group Captain Whitworth during his visit to RAF Scampton, 617 Squadron's base.

617 Squadron

At the time of Operation Chastise the Lancaster bomber was only just coming into service, but head of Bomber Command, Air Chief Marshal Arthur 'Bomber' Harris, was reluctant to withdraw a whole Lancaster squadron from the main force for the Dambuster mission. He decided to form a new squadron, manned with experienced crews who were coming off operations after completing their set number of missions. Wing Commander Guy Gibson, who had completed his tour with 109 Squadron, was asked to form the unit with experienced veterans who had completed two tours. In fact, only a third had completed their first tour. For some of the crew, the Dambusters raid was their first operational sortie.

While all the crew had flight experience, many of them suffered from air-sickness during training. They were accustomed to the smooth conditions at 10,000 feet, not the turbulence they would experience, attacking initially at 150 feet. This was later reduced to 60 feet when it was found that the casing of the bomb broke away if it was dropped above that height.

Altimeters are of little use at that height, so a novel method to accurately judge drops was devised. There was a spotlight under the nose and another behind the bomb bay door. They were angled so that, when the beams coincided, the plane was at the right height.

Left: Wing Commander Guy Gibson, standing next to the King, on his visit to 617 Squadron (the Dambusters), RAF Scampton, presenting members of the air crew to His Majesty.

Harris was furious. "I will not have aircraft flying about with spotlights on in defended areas," he protested. But there was no other way to judge the altitude accurately. As it was, two planes were damaged during practice by the water spout kicked up by the bomb when flying in too low.

The distance to the dam also had to be judged accurately. The Royal Aircraft Establishment came up with a Y-shaped bomb sight. The bomb aimer would look through an eyepiece at the foot of the Y. When a nail on the arms lined up with the towers at either end of the Möhne and Eder dams, the plane was 400 to 450 yards from the dam and the bomb was released. In fact, this did not work too well. It was difficult for the bomb targeter to hold the device steady in one hand as the plane bounced around. Instead, employing the same principle, they used marks on the perspex nose bubble and a piece of string.

Below: A group picture of 617 Squadron, the 'Dambusters', taken at Scampton, with one of the many Lancasters used in the raid visible just behind the men.

Left: *Lancaster, ED825/G, at Boscombe Down, Wiltshire, during handling trials. One of some 20 aircraft specially built to carry the Upkeep weapon on Operation Chastise and delivered to 617 Squadron as a spare aircraft.*

During the pre-flight checks, American Flight Lieutenant Joe McCarthy found that his Lancaster, call sign AJ-Q 'Queenie', was leaking coolant from the outer starboard engine and would not be able to fly. Fortunately, there was a spare plane, AJ-T 'Tommy', that had been flown that afternoon. It was already loaded with bombs in case of breakdowns. Transferring the crew to the other plane would take a little time and 'Tommy' would take off half an hour after the main force.

Left: *Members of 617 Squadron, the crew of Lancaster ED285/AJ-T sitting on the grass, posing under stormy clouds. Left to right: Sergeant G Johnson; Pilot Officer D A MacLean, navigator; Flight Lieutenant J C McCarthy, pilot; Sergeant L Eaton, gunner. In the rear are Sergeant R Batson, gunner; and Sergeant W G Ratcliffe, engineer.*

Guy Gibson VC

Wing Commander Guy Gibson was awarded the Victoria Cross for the courage he showed leading the Dambuster raids. After the action, he was sent on a lecture tour of the United States, where he was made a Commander of the Legion of Merit by President Franklin Roosevelt. He returned to duty in 1944. On 19 September, he was leading a raid as a Pathfinder master bomber when his Mosquito crashed and he was killed. He was just 26.

Barnes Wallis said of Gibson: "For some men of great courage and adventure, inactivity was a slow death. Would a man like Gibson ever have adjusted back to peacetime life? One can imagine it would have been a somewhat empty existence after all he had been through. Facing death had become his drug. He had seen countless friends and comrades perish in the great crusade. Perhaps something in him even welcomed the inevitability he had always felt that before the war ended he would join them in their Bomber Command Valhalla. He had pushed his luck beyond all limits and he knew it. But that was the kind of man he was…a man of great courage, inspiration and leadership. A man born for war…but born to fall in war."

Air Marshal 'Bomber' Harris called him: "As great a warrior as this island ever produced."

Below: Members of 617 Squadron with the unfortunately named 'Nigger', Wing Commander Guy Gibson's black Labrador dog. Nigger was run over, and died the night Gibson was due to bomb the dams. Nigger was buried at RAF Scampton where his grave is tended regularly (below).

Bottom: Half-length portrait of Wing Commander Guy Gibson wearing flying kit, while Commanding Officer of 617 Squadron.

Just after 2100 hours, the mission's leader, Wing Commander Guy Gibson, gave the signal to go. The red light went on, and the 52 Merlin engines on the 13 Lancasters of the first two waves roared into action. At 2128 hours, a green Aldis light flashed from the control tower and AJ-E 'Easy', piloted by Flight Lieutenant Barlow, rolled down the grass runway with the rest of the second wave. The four would be taking off first because they were taking a longer, more northerly route to the target.

As the pilots opened up their powerful Rolls-Royce Merlin engines, the four Lancasters lifted off over the northern boundary fence of RAF Scampton, 4 miles north of Lincoln, and turned towards the North Sea. Ten minutes later, the first wave rolled out.

Left: *Wing Commander Gibson and his crew board their Avro Lancaster AJ-G (ED 932/G) for the Dams raid. Left to right: Flight Lieutenant R D Trevor-Roper DEM; Sergeant J Pulford; Flight Sergeant G A Deering RCAF; Pilot Officer F M Spafford DFM RAAF; Flight Lieutenant R E G Hutchinson DFC; Wing Commander Guy Gibson; Pilot Officer H T Taerum RCAF.*

The nine second-wave aircraft, led by Gibson's AJ-G, took off in three groups of three, 10 minutes apart. A third wave of five Lancasters, acting as a backup, followed $2^{1}/_{2}$ hours later.

Over the North Sea, they checked their weapons and equipment. A strong wind blew Gibson and his lead flight of three off course. They crossed the Dutch coast right over a nest of anti-aircraft batteries, but escaped without loss or damage. They were still off course as they crossed from Holland into Germany, attracting the attention of searchlights and ack-ack fire. Flight Lieutenant Hopkin's plane was hit in the wing. He brushed over tree tops and under high tension cables, struggling to keep the Lancaster in the air as he headed on towards the target. The flak was so intense that Gibson broke radio silence to warn the others.

Below: Oblique view of the scale briefing model of the Möhne dam and its surrounding area.

The second flight of the first wave also encountered flak near Dülmen. The third flight was delayed by stronger headwinds and were behind schedule when they crossed into Germany. AJ-B, piloted by Flight Lieutenant Astell, turned over the canal at Rosendaal and followed it, apparently trying to check his position. Flying low to avoid searchlights and flak, he hit an electricity pylon 3 miles southeast of Marbech. The Lancaster reared up, burst into flames, then crashed to the ground. Two minutes later the bomb load exploded and all seven crew were killed.

Above: A view of the Möhne dam taken before the war, seen from an easterly direction, and a close-up view of one of the large towers (right).

Gibson arrived over the reservoir behind the Möhne dam at 0015 hours. He assembled his Lancaster in an anti-clockwise holding pattern and tried to raise AJ-B on the radio, not knowing that Astell and his men were already dead. Assessing the target and its defences, Gibson saw that it had three light flak batteries on the dam wall and three more in the valley. Gibson got on the radio and assigned five of the first wave's remaining eight Lancasters to the attack. The attack, he said, would be made as planned.

The Möhne dam was going to be attacked using the rotating bouncing bombs developed by the aircraft engineer Barnes Wallis. As Gibson prepared for his run in, the bomb was spun round up to speed by his weapons officer.

First Gibson made a dummy run to get the lie of the land. Although they attracted light flak, it was a cloudless, moonlit night – perfect conditions for the attack – and he reported by radio that he "liked the look of it". The attack run had been planned to allow the Lancasters time to check their direction, height and speed before crossing a spit of land that jutted out into the lake where they became visible to the flak gunners.

Gibson's Lancaster turned out of the holding pattern again and came in over the landmark spit of land towards the rear of the dam. The flak gunners, now alerted, were surprised to see spotlights on the darkened plane come on, making it an easy target. But these were vital to the mission. The bomb had to be dropped at precisely the right height. Light from the angled spots allowed the bomb targeter to judge the altitude of the plane.

Above: An aerial reconnaissance photograph of the Möhne dam before the raid. The Möhne and Sorpe dams provided 75 per cent of the water supplies for the Ruhr Valley industrial complex.

Left: This ingenious device was made to tell the bomb targeter when to drop the bomb. He would look through the hole at one end. When the two nails were aligned with the two towers of the Möhne dam, the bomb would be dropped. Unfortunately, it was hard to use in a plane bouncing in the turbulence of low-level flight.

As the Lancaster inched down to 60 feet, the bomb was spinning at 500 revs per minute backwards in the belly of the Lancaster. At 0028 hours, when the Lancaster was 450 feet from the Möhne dam, bomb targeter Pilot Officer Spafford pressed the release. The rear gunner Flight Lieutenant Trevor Roper watched it bounce three times across the surface of the lake before hitting the dam and sinking down. Moments later, when the bomb reached a depth of 30 feet, it exploded, throwing a vast column of water into the air, obscuring the dam. The bomb had struck the dam just 150 feet off centre, but the structure held. Gibson's wireless operator, Flight Lieutenant Hutchinson, sent in the signal "Goner 68A" in Morse code back to the flight controllers at Grantham in Lincolnshire. This meant that the bomb had gone off within 5 yards of the Möhne dam, but it had not been breached.

Above: *Aerial reconnaissance photograph, showing the breach in the Möhne dam caused by 617 Squadron's raid on 16/17 May 1943. The Eder dam was breached in the same operation by means of 'bouncing' bombs designed by Dr Barnes Wallis. This spectacular feat of precision bombing had tremendous propaganda value, although its practical consequences were less great than some had hoped.*

Gibson waited a few minutes for the water to settle before ordering Flight Lieutenant Hopgood in AJ-M into the attack. By that time AJ-N and AJ-Z had arrived. As AJ-M commenced its run-in, the spotlights again provided the waiting flak gunners with an easy target. A shell pierced the inner port wing fuel tank and the port outer engine caught fire. There was damage to the port inner engine as well, then the starboard wing was hit. In the heat of the action, the bomb was dropped just a few seconds late; it bounced and flew over the top of the dam. It fell down the front of the dam wall, before exploding beside the power generating house, destroying it. The plane was caught in the blast, and the Lancaster was now engulfed in flames. It climbed to about 500 feet. The tank exploded and the starboard wing fell off, sending the plane into a dive. It crashed and exploded near the village of Ostonnen, 4 miles northwest of the dam, where there is now a memorial.

Remarkably, not everyone was killed in the crash. With the port engine knocked out, the hydraulics failed and the rear gunner, Pilot Officer Tony Burcher, had to crank his turret around by hand to escape. He crawled into the rear fuselage, where his parachute was stored. As he strapped it on he saw the wireless operator, Sergeant John Minchin, seriously wounded, crawling down towards him. Burcher pushed Minchin out of the rear door, pulling the rip cord of his fellow crew-member's parachute as he fell. The plane was now coming down. Fearing it was too low, Burcher opened his parachute inside the plane, threw the canopy out of the door and let it pull him clear of the doomed Lancaster. He left the plane as the wing sheared off, then he passed out. The bomb targeter, Flight Sergeant Fraser, had managed to escape from the falling Lancaster in the same way, allowing the parachute to pull him clear via the front escape hatch.

When AJ-M plunged into the ground, the rest of the crew – Hopgood, Earnshaw, Brennan and Gregory – were killed instantly. Burcher came round on the ground, but had sustained serious back injuries from either hitting the tail of the plane or landing heavily. He and Fraser were taken prisoner. Minchin's parachute had failed to open in time to save him. He was buried, along with the other four dead crewmen, at the war cemetery at Rheinberg.

Gibson, who was now directing the attack by radio, called in Flight Lieutenant Micky Martin, who was an expert on low flying. Hoping to avert the disaster of Hopgood's AJ-M, Gibson flew alongside Martin's AJ-P to draw off some of the flak. His bomb dropped at the perfect point, but veered off to the left and exploded some 20 yards short. It blew another huge plume of water high in the air. The crew thought the dam had broken, but when the water subsided they saw that it was still intact. The message "Goner 58A" was sent back to Grantham, meaning that a bomb exploded 50 yards from Möhne dam, but it had not been breached.

As Martin's Lancaster swooped over the dam, it was hit by 20mm shells, damaging the ailerons and the starboard outer fuel tank, which was, fortunately, empty. Despite the damage, the Lancaster was still robust enough to limp the 400 miles back to base.

Next into the attack was Squadron Leader 'Dinghy' Young's AJ-A. Martin's Lancaster was still airworthy enough to fly parallel with Young's. Martin ordered his gunners to take on the flak towers. Their guns had been loaded with daytime tracer ammunition, which made the fire appear much heavier than it actually was. Meanwhile, Gibson

Left: *A view showing the breach in the Möhne dam with water flooding down the Ruhr Valley.*

turned his navigation lights on and flew over the dam from the south to draw the flak away. Young's attack was spot on. The bomb bounced three times, sank down next to the dam wall and exploded, throwing up a tremendous plume of water. Again the crew thought that the dam had gone, but when the water subsided they saw that it was still intact. The message "Goner 78A" was sent back to Grantham, who were now in despair. Three good hits had been made on the dam, but still it had not been breached. Barnes Wallis had led them to believe that one good hit would be enough.

But the Dambusters were not about to give up, and Gibson ordered Flight Lieutenant Maltby and AJ-J in for a fifth attack. Gibson and Martin flew on either side to divert the flak. As Maltby was coming in he noticed that the top of the dam was beginning to crumble. It seemed that Young's bomb had done the job, but Maltby was now committed. His bomb was dropped with perfect positioning. A plume of water shot to over 1,000 feet into the air before falling back into the lake. Still the dam did not collapse. Another failure message was sent back to Grantham, and Gibson ordered Flight Lieutenant Shannon's AJ-L in for a sixth attack.

However, as Shannon was lining up for the run in, the main wall of the dam suddenly crumbled and collapsed spectacularly. Millions of gallons of water burst through the 100-yard breach. The anti-aircraft fire abruptly ceased. Shannon was called off, and news of the success was transmitted back to Grantham while the Lancasters circled the disintegrating dam, admiring their handiwork.

Above: A vertical
reconnaissance photo
of the Ruhr Valley at
Froendenberg-
Boesperde, some
13 miles south of the
Möhne dam, showing
massive flooding
and the devastating
aftermath of the
bombing raids.

Maltby and Martin then set course for home, while Gibson accompanied the three Lancasters still carrying their bombs towards the Eder dam. Young went too, as he was to take over as mission leader if Gibson was shot down. The Eder was about 12 minutes' flying time away. There was no opposition on the way. However, the dam was difficult to locate as it was surrounded by similar wooded valleys filled with early morning mist.

Having located the target, the Lancasters began to circle. This time they would face no flak since the dam was undefended. However, the terrain was much more difficult, due to the shape of the valley. The Lancasters would have to approach over Waldeck Castle, which sat on top of a 1,000-foot peak. They would then have to dive down to the lake, turn 90 degrees to the left, 'hop' over a spit of land and quickly drop to 60 feet for a short run to the rear of the dam. As soon as they released their bombs, they would then have to pull up steeply to avoid the high ground on the other side of the dam. The approach was so tight that they would have no more than 5 seconds to line up the plane and release the weapon before it was too late.

Right: A reconnaissance photo of the Eder dam taken before the raid, and an oblique view of the scale briefing model of the Eder dam and the surrounding area (below right).

Shannon, in AJ-L, made three unsuccessful attempts but he could not get the right angle or the right height, so Gibson put him into the holding pattern and called on Squadron Leader Maudslay in AJ-Z. He also had problems getting into position. After two attempts, Gibson told him to hold off and sent Shannon back in. He made two unsuccessful further attempts, but on the third he lined up well and dropped his bomb. It bounced twice and exploded against the dam, sending a column of water 1,000 feet into the air, but without producing any visible damage whatsoever. The dam held and "Goner 78B" was sent to Grantham, meaning a bomb had exploded against the Eder dam, but it had not been breached.

Maudslay then came in again. On his second approach, Pilot Officer Fuller released the bomb slightly too late, to disastrous effect. It hit the dam's parapet and exploded with a brilliant flash, lighting up the valley for miles around. Although Maudslay had cleared the dam when the bomb exploded, the explosion was right behind him and he was caught in the blast. Gibson radioed him and asked if he was OK. Maudslay was heard to reply faintly, "I think so". There was some speculation that AJ-Z had been hit on the journey out, as something appeared to be hanging beneath it.

Left: *A reconnaissance photo showing the breach in the Eder dam. The awkward approach to the dam resulted in the failure of the first three attempts to place a bomb accurately enough to destroy it. However, the fourth aircraft to attack (AJ-N) was successful.*

Maudslay turned his damaged Lancaster for home, but was shot down by light flak at 0236 hours at Netterden, 2 miles east of Emmerich on the Dutch border and 75 miles from Eder. Maudslay and all of his crew were lost, and are buried in the Reichswald Forest war cemetery.

Gibson called up Astell in AJ-B, whose fate he still did not know. When he did not reply, he called on Flight Lieutenant Les Knight in AJ-N, who was carrying the last of the first wave's bouncing bombs. Knight made one dummy run on the dam to get a feel for the approach. On his second run, he lined the Lancaster up perfectly and bomb aimer Flight Officer Ed Johnson dropped the bomb on time. The bomb skipped over the lake three times and hit the wall near the centre. Knight opened the throttles and stood the Lancaster on its tail to clear the high ground on the far side of the dam. Again the bomb threw up a huge column of water, but this time it had punched a hole right through the middle of the dam. The top of the dam collapsed as a gigantic torrent of water burst through the fractured wall. The Eder was the largest dam in Europe. It held back a reservoir 17 miles long, and it was estimated that this initial cascade released 1.8 million gallons of water per second. As the Eder valley was steeper than the Möhne, the tidal wave sweeping down the valley was even more spectacular. Gibson signalled the codeword 'Dinghy' back to Grantham, meaning the Eder dam had been breached. The Eder power house was also destroyed.

Below: A vertical reconnaissance photo of the town of Kassel, some 30 miles downstream of the Eder dam. Large areas of water lie adjacent to the River Fulda which bisects the town.

Shannon and Knight went directly home, while Squadron Leader Young's AJ-A returned to inspect the damage to the Möhne dam with Guy Gibson. After that, radio contact was lost. AJ-A was shot down by flak north of Ijmuiden on the Dutch coast at 0258 hours, killing the entire crew, who are buried in the cemetery at Bergen. Gibson made it safely home, landing at 0415 hours.

The second wave of Lancasters had crossed the Dutch coast at almost the same time as the first wave. However, when passing over Vlieland, AJ-W, piloted by Flight Lieutenant Les Munro, was hit by flak that knocked out its radio. As this meant that Munro would not be able to direct the attack on the target, he returned to base, still carrying his bomb load.

Above: A vertical, aerial reconnaissance photograph, taken over the Eder dam in Germany, two months after the raid. The reservoir (Edersee) is completely dry and, on the river bed in front of the breached dam (top right), a light railway has been constructed in preparation for its repair. A new encampment of huts for workmen has also been built to the right of the dam.

AJ-K, flown by Sergeant Byers, was brought down crossing the Dutch coast at Texel at around 2300 hours. It was flying at around 300 feet and seems to have been downed by a lucky hit from a 10.5cm flak gun, depressed to its lowest level, although 20mm light flak may have been responsible. The aircraft crashed in the waters of the Waddensee west of Harlingen, killing all of the crew. The bomb did not go off at the time, but exploded four weeks after the crash, causing much surprise to the locals. One crew member, Sergeant McDowell, is buried in Harlingen cemetery. The rest have no known graves.

It seems that the spotlights used to keep the Lancaster 60 feet about the water were misaligned on AJ-H. Flying Officer Geoff Rice misjudged his height and touched the sea. The aircraft was engulfed in water, which ripped the bombs out of the belly of the Lancaster. Somehow Rice managed to keep the aircraft in the air. As he started to climb, the huge amount of water scooped into the fuselage by the drop all ran to the rear and poured out of the back of the plane, almost drowning Sergeant Burns, the rear gunner. With just two engines working, the Lancaster made it back to Scampton.

Although AJ-E, piloted by Flight Lieutenant Barlow, hugged the ground on the outward journey it was hit by flak, then ran into an electricity cable near Rees on the Rhine. It burst into flames and hit the ground a few hundred yards further on. Barlow and all of his crew died in the crash. Among the dead was Sergeant Liddell, who was 18 and must have lied about his age when he joined the RAF. The bomb did not go off. It bounced free and was examined by German bomb disposal experts the following morning.

Left: *A German official in civilian clothes standing by the 'Upkeep' weapon (Bouncing Bomb) salvaged from Flt Lt R N G Barlow's Avro Lancaster, ED927/G AJ-E. The Lancaster struck an electricity pylon and crashed 3 miles (5 km) east of Rees, near Haldern, Germany, at 2350 hours on 16 May, while flying to attack the Sorpe dam. Barlow and his crew were all killed.*

This meant that four of the five Lancasters that made up the second wave never made it to their target, the Sorpe dam. However, despite his late take-off, American Flight Lieutenant Joe McCarthy, flying AJ-T, did make it to the target. The compass deviation caused by the large metallic casing of the bouncing bomb in the belly of the Lancaster meant that the target was difficult to locate. There was fog in the valleys surrounding the reservoir, but visibility of the dam itself was good.

Left: An oblique view of the scale briefing model of the Sorpe dam.

For the attack on the Sorpe dam, they were not going to rotate the bombs and use its skipping properties as, due to the position of the dam in the valley, it was not possible to get a sufficient run at its rear. Instead they were to fly along the dam and drop it unspun like a conventional bomb. However, McCarthy's approach was hampered by a small hill at either end of the dam, and the spire of the village church that impeded his turn into the bomb run. The reserve plane was not fitted with spotlights to judge the height, so they dropped the bomb as best they could. It hit the dam and exploded, and part of the parapet was seen to crumble. AJ-T then returned to Scampton, though it had a little trouble landing as light flak had punctured one of its tyres.

It was not until almost 2 hours later that the third wave turned up at the Sorpe dam. AJ-F piloted by Flight Sergeant Ken Brown shot up a train on the way to the target. When he arrived at around 0300 hours, the fog had closed in, so he dropped some incendiaries in some trees. He then used the resulting fire as a landmark. While flames burnt the fog off, the bomb was dropped. It hit the dam and exploded at almost the same place as McCarthy's, but the structure appeared to hold. Brown then turned for home, flying over the Möhne dam where his gunners exchanged fire with one of the remaining flak nests. Near Hamm the aircraft came under heavy flak fire and the Lancaster returned home riddled with holes.

On its way out to attack the Lister Dam, a secondary target, AJ-C was hit by local 20mm gun fire just north of Hamm. The starboard inner engine burst into flame and the hydraulic system was knocked out. As the Lancaster plunged to the ground, the pilot, Pilot Officer Warner Ottley, said over the intercom: "I'm sorry boys, they got us." As the plane hit the ground, the tail section broke away from the main part of the aircraft and was flung free. In it was Sergeant Fred Tees. He was the front gunner but had exchanged places with Sergeant Harry Strange in the rear turret. Tees was the only survivor and was taken prisoner. When he died in 1982, he was cremated and his ashes were placed alongside the graves of the rest of the Lancaster's crew.

Below: The Möhne dam, as it was found by the 79th Division of the 9th US Army, when they overran the Ruhr in 1945. The dam had been hastily repaired by a workforce of some 7,000 men and was operational within four months of the raid.

Lancaster AJ-S, flown by Pilot Officer Louis Burpee, did not make it to the target either. The plane had drifted slightly off course over Holland. In an attempt to get back on course, Burpee was following the Wilhelmia Canal and flew too close to the night fighter base Gilze-Rejen at around 0200 hours. Although the flak defences did not have time to open up, a single search light dazzled the pilot. He flew through some trees, then into the ground. The aircraft exploded, followed a few seconds later by the bomb.

AJ-O under Flight Sergeant Townsend found what he thought was the Ennepe dam, another secondary target, around 0330 hours. It was shrouded in mist, but after three runs he dropped his bomb and returned over Holland in broad daylight, landing safely at 0615 hours. Post-war research has shown that he actually hit the nearby Bever dam, not the Ennepe, after fragments of the bomb were recovered.

There was one more flight that night. Flight Sergeant Anderson in AJ-Y was unable to locate the Sorpe dam due to the fog and returned home. Another Lancaster had made an 800-mile round trip across hostile territory unscathed.

The wall of water that swept down the Ruhr and Eder valleys killed at least 1,500 people, flooded factories, mines and steelworks, and forced those who had survived to flee to higher ground. The Dambusters raid may not have significantly dented Nazi Germany's armaments production, which continued to rise, and therefore may not have won the war. The Germans had already lost the battle of Stalingrad and would soon be in full retreat in the east. But the Allied landings of Normandy were still to come and the Lancaster bomber had shown, once again, that the British were not about to be defeated.

Above: Debriefing of Wing Commander Guy Gibson's crew. Squadron Leader Townson, Intelligence Officer, questions, from left to right: Spafford, Taerum and Trevor-Roper. Pulford and Deering are partly hidden. Air Chief Marshal Sir Arthur Harris and the Hon Ralph A Cochrane, Air Officer Commanding the Group, observe.

Why the Lancaster?

During World War II, Bomber Command's aim was to destroy as much of Germany's industry as possible. By denying the enemy armaments, it cut their effectiveness as a fighting force. However, it was discovered that, after a raid, the Germans were able to quickly rebuild factories, and the new plants were dispersed over a wide area, making any subsequent raids less effective. Consequently, the idea of attacking the power plants arose. As several factories used one source of power, if you knocked it out, you could disrupt a whole industry.

Aeronautical engineer Neville Barnes Wallis came up with the idea of hitting the dams of the Ruhr Valley early in the war. This, he believed, would deprive the Germans of armaments and bring the war to an early conclusion with far fewer casualties than there would have been otherwise. But there was a problem. Until the Lancaster was introduced in 1942, British bombers could not reach the Ruhr.

Conventional bombing would also be ineffective against the dams. Early in the war, bombs typically had only a one-in-three chance of landing within 5 miles of the target, and it was estimated that over 5,000 bombs would have to be dropped on the target to have any reasonable chance of breaching a dam. At the time, Bomber Command could not mount a raid of that scale.

Below: Armourers prepare to load an 8,000lb 'Super cookie' HC bomb into a waiting Lancaster.

Barnes Wallis

Barnes Wallis came up with the idea of dropping one massive bomb from a great height, which would cause it to penetrate deep into the subsoil. Then, when it went off, it would create a shockwave so large that it would collapse the dam. He calculated that, if a 10-ton bomb dropped from 40,000 feet, landed within 150 feet (45.7m) of the dam, it would still manage to breach it. But not even the Lancaster could lift a 10-ton bomb and it could only fly at 24,500 feet. Barnes Wallis proposed building his own six-engined Victory bomber to perform the feat, but it would take at least two years to develop and the Air Ministry were unwilling to provide the resources. Plans for the Victory bomber were scrapped in September 1941.

Although Barnes Wallis's big bomb idea was not put into action on the Dambuster raid, he went on to develop the 5-ton Tallboy bomb for smashing U-boat pens and, in 1945, the 10-ton Grand Slam earthquake bomb.

After a rethink, Barnes Wallis decided that, if he could not deliver a huge bomb from a great height, a smaller bomb would have to be delivered with great accuracy. After experiments on models, he undertook a full-size test, blowing a 30 by 180-foot hole in the disused Nant-y-Gro dam in Wales. From that, he worked out that it would be possible to breach the Möhne dam with just 7,500lb of explosives, well within the lift capacity of the Lancaster that was coming into service early in 1942.

Left: *Front view of a scale model of the Möhne dam photographed in 1954. The model was constructed in 1941 at the Garston Building Research Station. It was built to facilitate the testing of underwater explosive devices and was a 1:50 scale model of the actual target.*

The Victory Bomber

Barnes Wallis believed that a 10-ton bomb could not only take out the Ruhr dam but also systematically destroy the German industrial infrastructure but when the Lancaster bomber first came into service, it could not carry such a bomb load, so he came up with his own design for the Victory bomber. The specification was for a 50-ton bomber that could drop a 10-ton bomb from 45,000 feet and travel at 320 mph for 4,000 miles. To reach that height, the crew compartment would have to be pressurized. Defensive armament could be kept to a minimum. The bomber would be able to climb over Britain where RAF fighters could protect it. Once at its cruising altitude, enemy interceptors would not be able to reach it. However, it would be fitted with a four-gun turret in the tail, just in case.

It was to be 96 feet (29.3m) long with a wingspan of 172 feet (52.4m) and powered by Rolls-Royce Merlin or Bristol Hercules super-charged piston engines. It would use the same geodetic construction Barnes Wallis had developed for the Wellington bomber. This had proved durable and Vickers was tooled up to make it.

However, the Air Ministry was not keen on a plane that would only drop one bomb. They wanted a more flexible bomb and withdrew their support in 1942. Barnes Wallis continued with the idea of an earthquake bomb, with the smaller 12,000lb Tallboy bomb, and then the larger 22,000lb Grand Slam bomb. These were carried by Lancasters whose performance improved markedly during the war.

Left: Half-length portrait of Dr Barnes Wallis, sitting in a chair holding a model of a deep-penetration bomb. Only the Lancaster could carry these huge weapons.

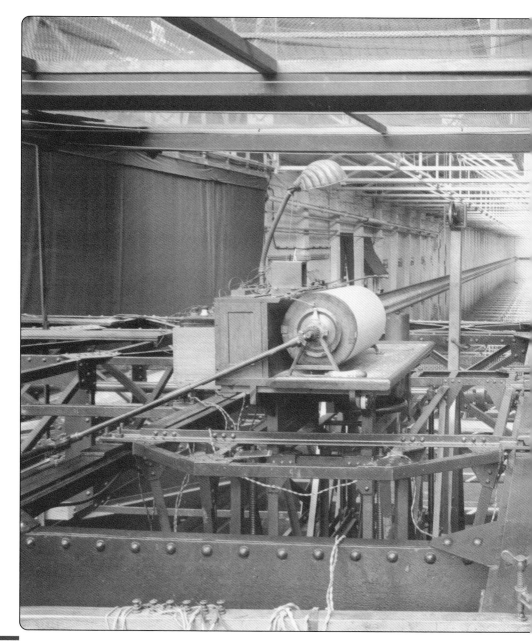

The Bouncing Bomb

Once the destruction of the Ruhr dams became a priority, a number of ingenious schemes were discussed. Missiles, radio-controlled aircraft packed with explosives, and special torpedoes that could cut their way through the torpedo nets in front of the dams were all mooted, along with suicide missions, parachuting commandoes carrying sacks filled with dynamite into the area. None were considered practical. Then the ever-inventive Barnes Wallis came up with the idea of the bouncing bomb. It was not a completely original concept. In the 16th and 17th centuries naval gunners found they could increase the range of their cannon balls by 'bouncing' them off the water like a stone in a pond. Early in the war pilots reported that bombs dropped short would still hit enemy shipping after skipping across the water. Barnes Wallis began experimenting with his daughter's marbles at his home in Surrey.

Then he moved to the 670-foot long water tank at the National Physical Laboratory ship testing facility at Teddington. He found that the critical angle for the ball to bounce was about 7 degrees.

Left: *A view of the large test tank in the Ship Research Department at the National Physical Laboratory in Teddington, England. The tank is 550 feet (167.6m) long, 30 feet (9.14m) wide and 12 feet (3.8m) deep. The carriage that runs along the length of the tank is capable of a maximum speed of 25 feet (7.6m) per second. The apparatus used to record data on the model during the test can be seen on the left of the photograph.*

Bouncing Bomb Sequence

Key to the effectiveness of the bomb was to get it to detonate at the right depth, against the face of the dam. To do that Barnes Wallis developed the concept of the bouncing bomb. Tests were performed off Chesil Beach using a Wellington bomber in December 1942. Barnes Wallis then wrote a paper called 'Attacks on Dams'. His ideas were dismissed by Air Chief Marshal Arthur 'Bomber' Harris, head of Bomber Command. It had been found that, for the bomb to skip effectively, it had to be spun. Harris feared the mechanism used to make the bomb rotate would tear one of his precious Lancasters apart. Even Barnes Wallis's superior, Vickers chairman Sir Charles Craven, ordered him to stop, but Barnes Wallis threatened to resign. However, Barnes Wallis was supported by the Chief of the Air Staff, Air Chief Marshal Sir Charles Portal and the Lancaster's designer Roy Chadwick, so Avro were told to give priority to work on Lancasters modified to carry the bouncing bombs.

Prior to the attack on the Möhne, Eder and Sorpe dams by 617 Squadron RAF on the night of 16/17 May 1943, much work needed to be done to make sure that the bomb would bounce correctly and hit the target exactly as calculated by Dr Barnes Wallis. Initially, there were problems with the bomb breaking up on impact with the water. Seen here is 617 Squadron during practice drops of the 'Upkeep' weapon at Reculver bombing range, Kent. The close-up is of Avro Lancaster ED932/G AJ-G being flown by Wing Commander Guy Gibson at low level over the camera crew.

Above: Here, the bomb rises from the water after its first 'bounce' during the second launch sequence. A group of observers (right) watch as the bomb bounces towards the shoreline. Dr Barnes Wallis can be seen on the extreme left of the group.

In order to achieve the seven-degree angle, the bombs would have to be dropped from a very low altitude. He also found that backspin improved the bounce. After three bounces, the bomb would decelerate enough so that it would sink at the wall of the dam and not overshoot. A bouncing bomb would skip over the torpedo nets, and the backspin would also help the bomb hug the dam wall, making the explosion more effective.

Above and left: *This dramatic picture shows the breach in the Möhne Dam, taken just four hours after the Dambusters raid in May 1943. The bomb that caused the damage was the same type as the one shown, cylindrical in shape and deadly when dropped at just the right height and speed.*

The German Bomb

The exact details of the bouncing bomb were an official secret until 1963. Indeed, the 1955 film *Dambusters* shows a spherical bomb, while the bombs used in the raid were cylindrical. This is ironic as the bomb from AJ-E, which crashed near Rees on its outward journey, had been thoroughly examined by German experts on the morning after the raid. On 17 June a report prepared by the minister of armaments and munitions, Albert Speer, was sent to Lüftwaffe chief Herman Göring, giving full details:

"The cylindrical bomb has no stabilizing fins. The diameter is 1,270mm and the length is 1,530mm. Each rim is secured with thirty bolts and strips of angle steel. The material used for the sides of the cylinder is 12.5mm thick whereas that used for the rims is 10mm thick. A high-explosive charge of some 2,600kg is made up of 41.7 per cent trinitroluol, 40.5 per cent hexogen and 17.5 per cent aluminium. The tubes for the three hydrostatic pistols, of the type used in anti-submarine depth-charges, each contain primer charges of 1,820kg of Tetryl. The self-destruction charge (intended to prevent an unexploded bomb being recovered if falling on land) consists of 1,255kg of Tetryl."

Plainly, that self-destruct device did not work.

Even though the Germans then knew the secrets of the bouncing bomb, it was of no consequence. The British only made 19 and they were never used again. However, the Germans developed their own version of the bouncing bomb, code-named Kurt, at the Luftwaffe Experimental Centre in Travemünde, for use against shipping. However, they had not cracked the secret of backspin and the project was discontinued in 1944.

Chapter Two

Roy Chadwick – Chief Designer

The genius behind the Avro Lancaster was Roy Chadwick. Born on 30 April 1893 at Farnworth near Widnes, Lancashire, he was in the fifth generation of engineers in his father's family. The eldest son of Charles Henry Chadwick, a mechanical engineer in Manchester, he went to school in Urmston. From his earliest years, Chadwick was fascinated with the idea of flying machines and made model gliders and aeroplanes.

At the age of 14, Roy Chadwick went to work in the drawing office of British Westinghouse. At night, he studied engineering at the Manchester College of Technology. He was determined to make his career in aeronautical engineering. When his apprenticeship at Westinghouse ended in December 1911, Chadwick joined the aircraft manufacturer A V Roe & Company Ltd and became personal assistant to the Manchester-born owner, A V Roe.

Above: Roy Chadwick was Avro's greatest designer. He was fascinated by the concept of flight from a very early age, and made his own models, which he would fly at night for fear of ridicule.

The Avro 504J was the most numerous trainer version to see service during World War I. It was normally powered by either an 80hp le Rhone or a 100hp Gnome Monosoupape engine. The photographs here were taken during an Allied aircraft demonstration in 1917. The A V Roe-designed 504J is seen being inspected and in flight.

He had a hand in the design of all the Avro 500 series of biplanes, including the World War I-vintage Avro 504, and in a number of experimental planes. Chadwick rose to head the design team and became chief designer in 1918, by which time he was recognized as one of the youngest, yet most experienced, aircraft designers.

In 1919, the world's first true light aircraft, the Avro Baby, sprang from Chadwick's drawing board. It was followed by the Avro Avian, used by Bert Hinkler to make the first solo flight from England to Australia in 1928. In 1931 Charles Kingsford Smith, another Australian air pioneer, purchased an Avro Avian, which he named the Southern Cross Minor, for an attempt to fly from Australia to England. He later sold the aircraft to Captain W N 'Bill' Lancaster, who vanished on 11 April 1933 over the Sahara Desert. Captain Lancaster's remains were found in 1962 and the wreck of the Southern Cross Minor is now in the Queensland Museum.

Right: *The first Avro Baby biplanes were powered by a water-cooled in-line Green engine of pre-1914 design. These had previously been installed in the Avro Type-D, but they were then thoroughly remodelled post-war by the Green Engine Company Ltd.*

Avro Baby

The Avro 534 Baby was a light, single-seater sporting biplane designed by Roy Chadwick. The prototype first flew on 30 April 1919, but crashed two minutes into the flight due to pilot error. The second prototype also crashed, seriously injuring Chadwick. However, on 31 May 1920, Avro's test pilot, Australian air-ace Bert Hinkler, made a non-stop flight in an Avro Baby from Croydon aerodrome to Turin – a distance of 655 miles – in 9 hours 30 minutes. On 11 April 1921, he flew a Baby non-stop from Sydney to his home town of Bundaberg 800 miles away, in 8 hours 40 minutes, setting a new distance record. Hinkler's Baby is preserved at the Queensland Museum in Brisbane. Another Baby made the first flight between London and Moscow in June 1922, and explorer Ernest Shackleton took a modified Baby with him on his final expedition to the Antarctic that year.

Powered by a 35-horsepower water-cooled Green engine, it had a top speed of 78 mph, a rate of climb of 500 feet a minute and a range of 240 miles. It was 17 feet 6 inches long, with a wingspan of 25 feet.

Left: *Roy Chadwick standing proudly next to the Avro 534 Baby prototype. This was taken at Hamble, England, in 1919.*

Left: The final version of the Baby was the type 554 Antarctic Baby, built as a photographic aircraft for the 1921–22 Shackleton-Rowett Expedition to Antarctica. This had a 80hp (60kW) le Rhone engine, raised tailplanes, rounded wingtips and tubular steel struts, used to replace rigging wires to avoid the problems of tensioning them with gloved hands.

Below: The Avro Avian was originally designed as a wooden biplane but later developed into a steel-tube monoplane. Seen here is an Avian IVM with Hermes engine and steel tube fuselage. The Avian could be powered by a 105hp Cirrus Hermes I, or 100hp Armstrong Siddeley Genet Major. The Avian Mk III (inset right) used an 85hp Cirrus II engine, with modified engine mount and tubular steel struts; approximately 33 were built.

The Avro Avian

The Avro 581 Avian prototype was built for the *Daily Mail* light aeroplane trials in Kent in September 1926. It had a wooden fuselage and was powered by a 70-horsepower Armstrong Siddeley Genet engine. This failed during the trials and was replaced by an 85-horsepower ADC Cirrus engine. The new plane, the Avro 581E, was sold to Bert Hinkler, who used it for his 15-day solo flight from Croydon in England to Darwin in Australia.

The production aircraft was called 594. A version with a welded steel tube fuselage was produced in 1929 as the Avro 616 Avian IVM, which had a 105-horsepower Cirrus Hermes engine; some 190 of this version were built. A single Genet-powered Avian II was bought by the RAF. Avians were also bought by the South African Air Force, the Chinese Naval Air Service, the Estonian Air Force and the Royal Canadian Air Force. They were also made in the United States and Canada. Air-ace Amelia Earhart used an Avian on her first solo return flight across the North American continent in August 1928.

Right: Avro 594 Avian Mk 4A, G-ABCF 'Southern Cross Junior', was the aircraft used by Australian Sir Charles Kingsford Smith, a great aviation hero, to make his prize-winning solo flight from England to Australia in 1930.

Chadwick's Champion

The Avian IVM could take a crew of two. It was 24 feet 3 inches long, with a wingspan of 28 feet. It had a top speed of 105mph and a range of 360 miles. Its rate of climb was 600 feet a minute and its ceiling was 12,500 feet. Champion pilot Bert Hinkler bought the race-winning aircraft and made a non-stop flight to Riga in Latvia in the same year, covering a total of 1,200 miles. Then in February of 1928, Hinkler made a spectacular solo flight to Australia in that same aircraft.

Below: Roy Chadwick, Bert Hinkler and R J Parrott standing beside Avian G-EBOV, in which Hinkler won three races in 1927 at Bournemouth, England.

Chadwick had designed the Avro Pike – Britain's first multi-role combat plane – during World War I. However, it did not progress beyond the prototype stage. He returned to designing military aircraft with the Avro Aldershot, the world's biggest single-engine bomber. It went into service with the RAF's 99 Squadron in 1924, but was replaced by the multi-engined Handley Page Hyderabad the following year.

Below: It was in early 1920 that Chadwick designed the world's biggest single-engine bomber, the Avro 549 Aldershot. The first prototype, J6852, is seen here at the A V Roe works in Hamble, England.

Right: *The Avro 621 Tutor was a two-seat, radial-engined biplane, built in 1933. It was a simple but rugged initial trainer that was used by the RAF. In total, 380 Tutors were built and exported to seven countries. In a civilian version it was also sold to Australia and Tanganyika.*

The Avro Pike

The Avro 523 Pike was designed as a British multi-role combat aircraft by Roy Chadwick during World War I. The Royal Naval Air Service needed an anti-Zeppelin fighter that was also capable of both light bombing and long-range reconnaissance. The Pike was a large biplane, driven by two backward-facing pusher propellers. It had three open cockpits, the centre one being occupied by the pilot, with gunners manning .303 Lewis guns in the bays in front of and behind him. Two prototypes were produced; both were rejected by the Admiralty.

The Pike first flew in May 1916. It was 39 feet 1 inch long with a wingspan of 60 feet. Powered by two 160-horsepower Sunbeam Nubian engines, it had a maximum speed of 97mph, a rate of climb of 526 feet per minute and an endurance of seven hours. It could also carry two 112lb bombs in an internal bay.

Below: *The Avro 523 'The Pike' RNAS Serial N523 – the first Avro aircraft to receive a name. This aircraft was seen as a multi-role combat aircraft for use during World War I, but did not progress past the prototype stage. It was intended to provide the Royal Naval Air Service (RNAS) with an anti-Zeppelin fighter that was also capable of both long-range reconnaissance and light bombing.*

Below: Seen in flight here are two Avro 652A
Anson Mk Is. The Anson was originally designed
for maritime reconnaissance but soon became
obsolete. However, it was rescued from obscurity
by its suitability as a multi-engine air-crew trainer,
thus becoming the mainstay of the British
Commonwealth Air Training Plan.

The Avro Tutor replaced the Avro 504 in 1932 and was used as an RAF trainer in World War
II. In 1933, Chadwick designed the Avro 652 for Imperial Airways. This was soon converted
into the Avro Anson, a light bomber and transport plane that the RAF also used as a trainer.
Over 11,000 were built. Many World War II bomber crews were trained in Ansons in Canada.

Then the Air Ministry issued Specification P.13/36 for a twin-engined medium bomber for "world-wide use", powered by two Rolls-Royce Vulture engines. Chadwick developed a long-range, all-metal bomber built around a huge bomb bay, capable of holding 10 tons of bombs and mines, in any combination. For ease of production, the fuselage was made in five separate sections which could then be manufactured at different factories and assembled at Avro's giant assembly works at Woodford in Cheshire. The plane was named the Manchester. The prototype L7246 made its first flight in July 1939 and 207 Squadron received their first Manchesters in November 1940.

Above: *The Avro 652 was designed as a light, four-passenger civil transport and mail aircraft. The only two to be built had been ordered by Imperial Airways in 1934, and were registered G-ACRM c/n 698 and G-ACRN c/n 699. The first flew on 7 January 1935, and two months later both were delivered to Imperial Airways, who named them respectively, Avalon and Avatar. G-ACRN Avatar can be seen in the photograph.*

Below: *The first of two Manchester prototypes, L7246 flew on 25 July 1939 from Ringway Airport, England, piloted by Group Captain H A Brown. While only airborne for 17 minutes, it was long enough to demonstrate that the Vulture engines were putting out much less power than had been anticipated, and wing loading made the aircraft extremely difficult to fly. The prototype is seen here at Ringway.*

Left: Avro 679 Manchester prototype, with the Rolls-Royce Vulture engine installation.

From the beginning, it was clear that the Vulture engines were inadequate for the task. Chadwick had always wanted to use Rolls-Royce Merlin engines. He had already designed a four-engined version of the Manchester, and showed the Air Ministry how he could lengthen the Manchester's wing to carry four Merlin engines. The Air Ministry agreed to write a new specification for a four-engined bomber, and the Lancaster was born.

Above: *Avro 683 Lancaster nose production at Chadderton, England.*

Work got underway on the Avro Type 683 Manchester III – as the Lancaster was originally known – in November 1940. It first took to the air in January 1941. It was immediately evident that the soon to be Lancaster bomber was a highly successful aeroplane. It went straight into full production. Avro had 7 factories and 100 sub-contractors building Lancasters, thus employing 40,000 people. Thirty-five RAF squadrons were equipped with Lancasters, which could fly higher, carry heavier payloads and penetrate deeper into enemy territory than any other plane at that time.

But that was not the end of it. Chadwick's drawing office employed over 200 draughtsmen and tracers working on improvements. Each week, he would go around the office, looking at the work of each draughtsman. It was said that he could spot any mistake immediately and correct it. During the war he would work far into the night on the modifications for specific operations, including those on the Lancasters used on the Dambusters raid in 1943. He also designed the Avro Shackleton, York and Lincoln aircraft, which all saw service.

Left: *The Mk III Manchester BT308 had its maiden flight on 9 January 1941, and was essentially the first Lancaster, being powered by four Merlin engines and with increased wingspan. It initially retained the three fins and twin outboard rudders (the central fin had no movable control surface) of the Manchester I.*

Left: *Seen here in flight is Avro 696 Shackleton Mk I, VP256. The Shackleton was the first British bomber to feature contra-rotating propeller blades. It was used as a long-range maritime patrol aircraft.*

After the war, Chadwick went on to design the Lancastrian and the Tudor, the world's first pressurized civil airliner. However, problems beset the project. Orders were low and production was cut. But Chadwick never lost faith in his aeroplane, and the Tudor later proved its worth in the Berlin airlift of 1948–49. The Avro Ashton, a Royal Air Force research aircraft, was in fact a direct development of the Tudor.

Right: The Avro Lincoln was designed by Roy Chadwick as a four-engined heavy bomber for use in World War II. It first flew on 9 June 1944 and entered service in August 1945, which made it too late to be used in action. It was the last piston-engined bomber built for the RAF – the jet age had by now become a reality.

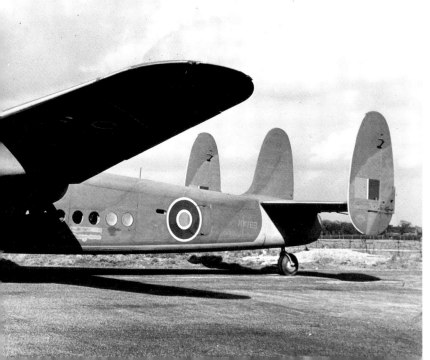

Left: The Avro York was a transport aircraft that was derived from the Lancaster bomber, and was used for both military and civilian roles between 1943 and 1964. Winston Churchill used a York, LV633, as his personal aircraft.

In an attempt to increase sales, Chadwick went to work on a larger version of the Tudor. On 23 August 1947 he went to Woodford for a test flight of the 60-seater Avro Tudor II. There had been an overnight service to the ailerons, and an error had been made in reassembling the controls. Just after take-off, Avro test pilot, Bill Thorn – who had also been the test pilot of the Lancaster – tried to turn to starboard. The port wing dipped. The engines cut and the plane crashed into a field beside the aerodrome. All would have been well, but there was a pond in the field, surrounded by trees. The plane ploughed into the trees, its nose broke off and the two pilots were drowned in the pond. Roy Chadwick, who had been standing behind the pilots in the cockpit, was flung out. He landed 60 yards away and died of a fractured skull.

Left: *The Lancastrian was designated a passenger and mail transport aircraft. It was very similar to the Lancaster, but differed primarily in having all of the armour and armament removed to save weight, and with the addition of streamlined metal fairings to replace the glazed fore and aft turrets. This modification of abundant military aircraft into desperately needed civil transports was common in the immediate post-war period.*

Below: *This Avro 688 Tudor 4, G-AHNN, belonged to British South American Airways (BSAA), a British state-run airline of the 1940s. Originally named British Latin American Air Lines (BLAIR), BSAA was split off from the British Overseas Airways Corporation to operate their South Atlantic routes.*

During his lifetime, Roy Chadwick designed some 40 successful aircraft and contributed to the development of many more. Although most of his designs were for war planes, his greatest hope was that the aeroplane would unite the people of the world. A visionary, he saw the huge potential of jet propulsion, but did not live long enough to exploit it. However, he did leave behind, in the hands of the Air Ministry, one final brilliant conception. This was the giant jet-powered delta-wing bomber – the Avro Vulcan, which was to become the RAF's front-line bomber for over 30 years.

The Vulcan Bomber

While Roy Chadwick never got to see the Avro Vulcan fly, the design concept was his. He began working on it in 1947, just before he died. It was built to Air Ministry Specification B.35/46 for a bomber with a top speed of 580 mph, an operating ceiling of 50,000 feet and a range of 3,950 miles, carrying a bomb load of 10,000lb. Three designs were approved – the Vickers Valiant, the Handley Page Victor and the Avro Vulcan.

What Roy Chadwick envisaged was a tailless, delta wing – practically one flying wing. It would be swept back to offset the transonic effects, with wingtip rudders for control. There were two bomb bays, one in each wing, and four engines, two at the front below the wing and two at the back above it. However, the Ministry did not like the revolutionary design and it was modified, giving the Vulcan a tail, a central fuselage and four conventionally-paired engines. The delta wing, then an unproven concept, was kept. The new design took to the air on 30 August 1952.

Left: Seen here in flight is the Avro 706 Ashton Prototype, WB490. The Avro Type 689 Tudor 9 was later renamed the Ashton and used as a four-jet engine research aeroplane, powered by Rolls-Royce Nene engines paired in wing nacelles.

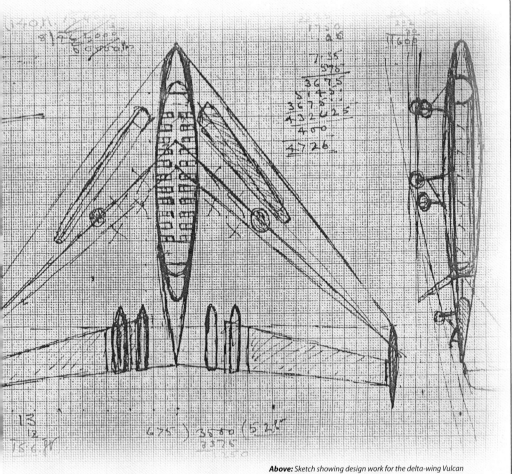

Above: Sketch showing design work for the delta-wing Vulcan (left), begun at A V Roe under the guidance of Roy Chadwick. Sadly he died before the project came to fruition.

Above: Sir Edwin Alliott Verdon Roe (left), seen here with his brother H V Roe, at an aircraft gathering in the early 1900s.

Right: The first advertisement for A V Roe & Company, featured in Flight *magazine on 1 January 1910.*

Chapter Three

A V Roe

One of Britain's first aircraft manufacturers, A V Roe & Company was established at Brownsfield Mills, Manchester, by Alliott Verdon Roe and his brother H V Roe on 1 January 1910. Alliott Roe had already made a name for himself as the first man in England to build and fly an aircraft.

Above: Assembly work being carried out on a
Type E Military biplane at Brownsfield Mill,
Manchester, England in 1912.

Right: A photograph used for A V Roe's pilot licence, with dates and city clearly marked.

Sir Alliott Verdon Roe

Born in 1877 in Manchester, Alliott Verdon Roe left school at the age of 15 and went to British Columbia where he became an apprentice in a locomotive works. Later he returned to England and studied marine engineering at King's College, London. He became a ship-board engineer, but became fascinated in how birds flew. Taking a job in the automobile industry, he spent his spare time making and flying models. After hearing of the Wright brothers' flight in 1903, he became fascinated by powered flight. In 1907, he entered the *Daily Mail* model aircraft competition at Alexandra Palace, beating 200 competitors to win the £75 prize. He used the money to build a full-size model of the plane in the hope of winning the £2,500 put up by Brooklands Automobile Racing Club for the first person to fly a circuit of their track. Unfortunately, his design had an underpowered engine and it did not get off the ground. However, he added a larger engine and made a number of short flights in June 1908. With his brother, Alliott built a triplane fitted with a 9hp JAP motorcycle engine that made a number of flights in 1909. This plane is now preserved in the Science Museum, South Kensington, London. His brother, the head of a manufacturing company in Manchester, then helped him set up A V Roe & Company in Manchester, which Alliott ran until 1928.

Above: A V Roe gets to grips with his original triplane, which was a flimsy affair due to lack of money. Where Roe would have liked to use metal parts, he had to make do with wood, which made the construction very flexible. Three wings were accompanied by a triplane tail. He originally used a 6hp JAP motorcycle engine but later changed to a 24hp Antoinette engine.

Right: Military personnel take time to look over the A V Roe 504J trainer, which the military used extensively during World War I.

On 8 June 1928, the twentieth anniversary of his first flight, Roe was given a dinner in recognition of his pioneer work for British aviation, and in 1929 he was knighted. In 1948, he was elected a fellow of the Royal Aeronautical Society, which he had joined almost 40 years earlier. He died in 1958.

In 1911, Roe's new company designed and built the world's first totally enclosed cabin monoplane. It first flew in 1912 and was entered in British military trials the same year. In October 1912 it established a British flying endurance record of $7^{1}/_{2}$ hours.

The following year, the company built the Avro 504, a wooden biplane that became the most well-known military aircraft of World War I. Three Avro 504s attacked the Zeppelin sheds at Friedrichshafen on 21 November 1914, the first organized air raid in the history of warfare. The Avro 504 was also the first plane to strafe troops on the ground. In 1917 it became the Royal Flying Corps' standard trainer and continued in service with the RAF for a quarter of a century. The design was so successful that most of the world's aircraft designers adopted its general layout. Some 8,340 aircraft were made at factories in Hamble, Failsworth, Miles Platting and Newton Heath over 20 years.

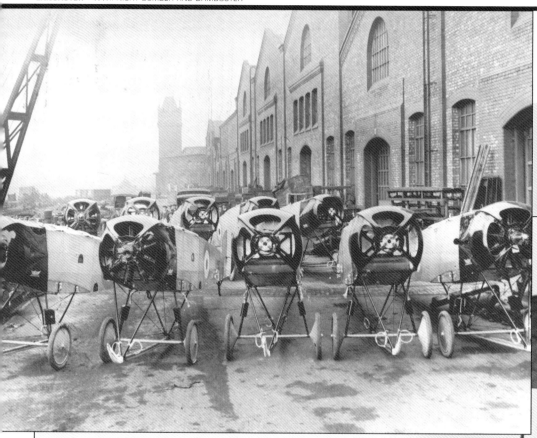

Avro 504

First flown on 18 September 1913, the two-bay Avro 504 was designed for training and private flying. It was made of wood and had a distinctive square-section fuselage. Immediately before the outbreak of World War I, a number were bought by the Royal Flying Corps and the Royal Naval Air Service. They were taken to France when war broke out, where, on 22 August 1914, one of the RFC aircraft became the first British aircraft to be shot down by the Germans. Another was shot down when the RNAS sent four 504s to bomb the Zeppelin works at Friedrichshafen on the shores of Lake Constance on 21 November 1914. Dropping four 20lb bombs each, they made several direct hits on the airship sheds and destroyed the hydrogen plant.

Left: A number of fuselages for the Avro 504J, sitting in the yard outside the Mather & Platts extension at Newton Heath in Manchester, England, waiting for final assembly.

Below: The prototype of the Avro 504 in its original form, seen here at Brooklands airfield in Weybridge, Surrey, England in 1913.

The 504 was soon obsolete as a frontline aircraft, but came into its own as a trainer. In the winter of 1917–18, some were converted to equip the RFC's Home Defence squadrons. These were single-seaters and had a Lewis gun above the wing.

After the war, they continued to be used as trainers and over 300 were sold off for civilian use, for pleasure flying and banner towing well into the 1930s. Training versions were sold to Chinese warlords, but were used to drop hand grenades and mortar shells as bombs.

In 1925, the 504N was developed, using the Armstrong Siddeley Lynx engine. It was used in RAF training schools and sold to Belgium, Brazil, Chile, Denmark, Greece, Thailand and South Africa. Versions were built under licence in Argentina, Australia, Denmark, Belgium, Canada, Japan and Mexico. In 1933, the RAF finally replaced the 504N with the Avro Tutor, although a small number continued in civilian use until 1940, when seven were taken back into RAF service and used for towing targets.

The 504 usually carried a crew of two. It was 29 feet 5 inches long with a wingspan of 36 feet. Its maximum speed was 90mph with a rate of climb of 700 feet a minute to a ceiling of 16,000 feet. It had a range of 250 miles. In all, more than 17,000 were made.

Below: An Avro 504J, B3168, seen at the School of Special Flying at Gosport Airfield in Hampshire during 1918. This is the same year that the newly formed Royal Air Force took over the airfield.

Above: *A trio of Avro 504Ns of 4FTS, based in Egypt, take their trainee pilots out for some flying experience.*

In the 1920s, Avro moved its test facilities from Alexandra Park Aerodrome in south Manchester to a rural site in the south of the city at New Hall Farm, Woodford in Cheshire. Having outgrown its Brownsfield Mills site, production was also moved to Woodford. The site is used by aircraft builders BAE Systems to this day.

Left: *An aerial view of the Woodford flight sheds, Manchester, taken in 1939. Avro moved here in 1924 after leaving Alexandra Park Aerodrome in Manchester. Although Woodford only had a small grassy airstrip at the time, it grew rapidly over the years and became home to A V Roe and then to its parent company BAE Systems.*

Right: The beautiful Hawker Hurricane, which never seemed to inspire quite the same following as the Spitfire. This is a Royal Navy version that can still be seen flying at many exhibitions and air shows.

In 1928, Roe sold a controlling interest in the firm to the Armstrong Siddeley Motor Company. Moving on, he bought into boat-builders Saunders Ltd of Cowes on the Isle of Wight and formed the Saunders-Roe company. There he developed flying boats, jet aircraft, helicopters and hovercraft.

In 1935, Avro became a subsidiary of Hawker Siddeley. That company itself had been formed that year when Hawker Aircraft bought the car company and engine-builder Armstrong Siddeley and the aircraft manufacturer Armstrong Whitworth Aircraft. Hawker Aircraft had started after World War I when the Sopwith Aviation Company, maker of the famous Sopwith Camel, went bankrupt. Sopwith test pilot Harry Hawker and three others, including Thomas Sopwith, bought the assets of Sopwith and formed H G Hawker Engineering in 1920. In 1934, they bought up the Gloster Aircraft Company.

Siddeley Autocars had started in 1902, making cars heavily based on the Peugeot. In 1905, it merged with Wolseley. The company was bought by Armstrong Whitworth, the industrial giant started by William George Armstrong in 1847. Its aviation division became Armstrong Whitworth Aircraft in 1920. This was bought by John Davenport Siddeley – founder of Siddeley Autocars – in 1927, when Vickers and Armstrong merged to form Vickers-Armstrong. He also bought the automotive division to form Armstrong Siddeley, which he sold on to Hawker Aircraft.

The constituent companies of Hawker Siddeley continued to produce their own designs under their own names, while sharing manufacturing work throughout the group. During World War II, Hawker Siddeley was one of the United Kingdom's most important aviation companies, producing among other things the Hawker Hurricane fighter plane.

Below: A general view inside the A V Roe, Newton Heath, assembly plant in Manchester. Shown here are people attending to different stages of the assembly of the 621 Tutor aircraft. This was an inter-war aircraft used extensively by the RAF, along with many other air forces around the world, as a basic trainer.

The Avro Tutor

The Avro 621 was designed by Roy Chadwick as a metal replacement for the Avro 504. Conceived as a pilot trainer, the biplane was powered either by a 155-horsepower Armstrong Siddeley Mongoose, or a 180-horsepower Armstrong Siddeley Lynx IV or 240-horsepower IVC engine. The Mongoose-powered version was called the 621 Trainer, while the more common Lynx-engined plane became the Tutor, which took to the air in 1930. It supplanted the 504 as the RAF's trainer in 1933, remaining in service until 1939. The Tutor also saw service in Australia, Canada, China, Czechoslovakia, Denmark, Iraq, Ireland, Greece, Poland and South Africa. Known for their good handling, they often featured at air shows.

The Tutor was 24 feet 4 inches long with a wingspan of 34 feet. It had a top speed of 120mph and a total range of 250 miles. It could climb at 910 feet per minute to reach a ceiling of 16,000 feet.

The Avro Anson

The Avro Anson began life as the Avro 652 – a civil airline commission by Imperial Airways in May 1933. Imperial's specification was for a four-seat passenger plane capable of flying 420 miles at a cruising speed of 130mph. Roy Chadwick produced a low-wing monoplane, powered by a pair of Armstrong Siddeley Cheetah V engines with landing gear that could be retracted manually.

In May 1934, the month after the first orders were made, the Air Ministry approached Avro, looking for a twin-engined landplane for coastal reconnaissance. By the end of the month, Chadwick's design team had come up with the 652A, a militarized version of the still-incomplete Avro 652.

The civil version first flew on 7 January 1935 and was delivered to Imperial Airways on 11 March. The military Avro 652A made its first flight on 24 March. In tests against the de Havilland D.H.89M, it proved to have longer range and endurance. The 652A went into production as the Avro Anson under Air Ministry specification 18/35. The first production aircraft flew on 31 December 1935 and only three months later it went into service with 48 Squadron. It was the RAF's first monoplane and its first plane with retractable landing gear. The only faster planes in the RAF were its top fighters.

The Mark I production version was powered by two 350-horsepower Armstrong Siddeley IX radial engines. It carried two machine guns – one fixed forward-firing Vickers gun in the nose and a Lewis gun in a dorsal turret. It could also carry two 100lb bombs under the wing centre section and eight 20lb bombs under the wings. Early in the war, Ansons were deployed with bomber squadrons until purpose-built aircraft arrived.

By 1941, the Anson had been withdrawn from coastal reconnaissance and anti-submarine patrols around the British coast, but continued in service as a trainer in Britain and in Canada. More than 3,000 Ansons were produced as trainers, over 2,800 of them in Canada. The Anson was recalled to Coastal Command service in 1943 for air-sea rescue squadrons. They were also used by communications and transport squadrons, often returning to their original passenger transport role. Special duties squadrons also used the Anson for anti-aircraft calibration, combined operations training, radar counter measures and wireless intelligence. The Anson remained in use as a light transport and communications aircraft until 1968.

The plane was 42 feet 3 inches long with a wingspan of 56 feet 5 inches. It had a top speed of 188mph at 7,000 feet, a ceiling of 19,000 feet and a range of 790 miles.

Below: *Named after the British Admiral George Anson, the Avro Anson was originally designed for maritime reconnaissance. Sadly it soon became obsolete, but made a comeback once it was known to be an ideal aircrew trainer.*

With the 504, Avro had developed a reputation for designing trainers. Building on this reputation, they produced the more robust Avro Tutor biplane in the 1930s that the RAF also bought in quantity. The twin-engined Avro Anson airliner followed, but as Europe began to re-arm, the firm returned to manufacturing combat aircraft. In World War II, they produced the Avro Manchester, Lancaster and Lincoln.

Below: *An Avro Tutor awaits its student pilot. These were used for training with the RAF, the marking of which can be seen clearly on the fuselage.*

Above: *Although also a civilian aircraft, the Avro Anson was used extensively by the RAF; this one is in use with 22 Squadron.*

Left: A rare aircraft indeed, is this Lancastrian prototype. Based on the Lancaster, the original conversion to civilian transporter took place at the A V Roe works in Canada, which produced three aircraft for use by Trans Canada Airlines (TCQ). Its success led to the aircraft being taken up by a number of different airlines around the world.

Below: Seen here is an Avro 691 Lancastrian IV, which belonged to Argentina.

Below: *This Avro 696 Shackleton in full flight is a Mk III version and has the wingtip fuel tanks fitted.*

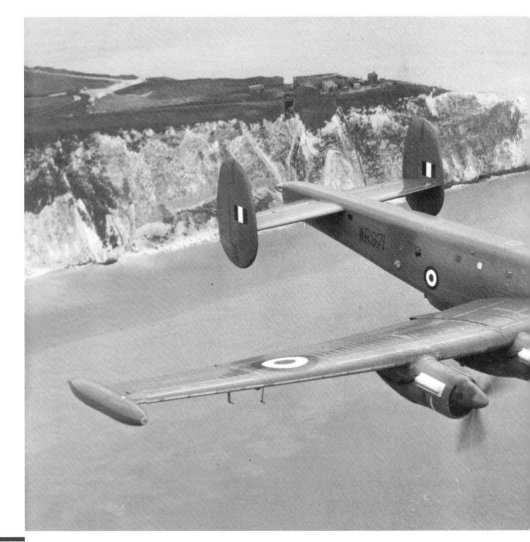

Above: *This photograph was taken at a great angle to see the airborne lifeboat attached to the underside of this 696 Avro Shackleton Mk I.*

After the war, the design of the Lancaster yielded the civilian Lancastrian and maritime reconnaissance Shackleton. They then came up with the Tudor which had the same wings and engines as the Lincoln. However, it had to compete with designs by Bristol, Canadair, Douglas, Handley Page and Lockheed. It first flew in June 1945, but following the cancellation of an order by the British Overseas Airways Corporation only 34 were made. The older Avro York was more successful, and both Tudors and Yorks played an important part in the Berlin airlift.

Avro went on to make Vulcan bombers, which were originally designed as a nuclear strike aircraft. They were armed with the Avro Blue Steel stand-off nuclear bomb. The Vulcan saw service as a conventional bomber during the British campaign to recapture the Falkland Islands in 1982.

Below: *General views of the assembly plant at Chadderton, England, during 1958. Shown here is the assembly of the main fuselage and wings and the nose production (left) of the huge Vulcan aircraft.*

Above: *The design for the Hawker Siddeley HS748 aircraft was started by Avro back in the late 1950s to replace the ageing Dakota DC3. The first example flew from Avro's Woodford plant on 24 June, 1960.*

The company also developed the twin turboprop Avro 748 airliner, powered by two Rolls-Royce Dart engines, in the 1950s. It sold well worldwide; the RAF and a number of Commonwealth countries bought a variant known as the Andover.

In the 1950s, the Hawker Siddeley Group bought the former Victory Aircraft firm in Malton, Ontario, and renamed it Avro Aircraft Limited (Canada). However, Avro Canada was a subsidiary of the Hawker Siddeley Group and only used the Avro name for trading purposes. When it was absorbed into Hawker Siddeley Aviation in 1963, the Avro name was dropped. However, the parent company British Aerospace marketed the BAe 146 as the Avro RJ – or regional jet – from 1994 to 2001. It was sometimes also known as the Avro 146. Meanwhile the design of the Avro 748 evolved into the BAe ATP – Advanced Turbo Prop.

Left: *The delta-wing Vulcan is an incredible aircraft and to see it taking off is awe-inspiring. The noise alone is enough to deafen anybody and ear protectors are definitely advised. The Vulcan was used during the Falklands War and caused considerable damage to the airstrip at Stanley by its precise bombing actions.*

A few Avro 504s, Tudors, Ansons and Lancasters are maintained in flying condition as part of Britain's aviation heritage. The Avro Shackleton remained in service with the RAF for 39 years. It held the record for the longest period of active service in the RAF by any plane until it was overtaken by the English Electric Canberra in 1998.

Below: *Hawker Siddeley started the design on the Avro RJ/BAe 146 project, when it was known as the HS 146. The economic downturn, due to the 1973 oil crisis, put the brakes on development, although it did continue on a small-scale basis. British Aerospace, Hawker Siddeley's corporate successor, continued the project and carried out the final work. The BAe 146, as it became, received its certificate of airworthiness on 8 February 1983.*

Above: *The BAe ATP was designed as an evolution of the Hawker Siddeley HS 748. The planners at British Aerospace believed there was a place in the market for a short-range, low-noise, fuel-efficient turboprop aircraft, and so the ATP was born. Unfortunately by the time it was on the market, it already had several established rivals and only 64 examples were made before production ceased.*

Right: The ground crew of 269 Squadron make the final adjustments to a Mark II Lifeboat, loaded to the belly of its parent aircraft, a Vickers Warwick ASR Mark I.

Below: A Warwick ASR (Air Sea Rescue) Mark I of 282 Squadron, based at St Eval, Cornwall, England. Seen here in flight and carrying the short Mark IA Lifeboat.

Chapter Four

On the Drawing Board

The Avro Manchester lays claim to being one of the least successful British aircraft of World War II. Only 209 were made and production ceased in November 1941. However, its final version, the Mark III Manchester, which took to the air in January 1941, was in essence the first Lancaster. Indeed, without the Manchester, there would have been no Lancaster, which turned out to be the best British bomber of the war.

The Manchester was developed in response to Air Ministry Specification P.13/36 issued on May 1936. This called for a twin-engined heavy bomber for "world-wide use", powered by the new Rolls-Royce Vulture engine that was still under development in 1936. The Vickers Warwick and the Handley Page Halifax were designed initially to the same specification.

Vickers Warwick

The Warwick was originally designed to Air Ministry Specification B.1/35 for a twin-engined medium bomber developed from the Vickers Wellington. After the prototype orders were cancelled in 1936, it was put forward under P.13/36 in competition with the Avro Manchester and the Handley Page Halifax. As required, the first prototype used the underpowered Rolls-Royce Vulture engine. A second prototype, utilising the Bristol Centaurus radial engine, flew on 5 April 1940. This proved more promising, but it was soon decided to use the American Pratt & Whitney Double Wasp radial engine. The converted prototype took to the air in July 1941.

The Warwick used the geodesic airframe construction Barnes Wallis pioneered in the Wellesley and Wellington. Fabric was wired over a network of intersecting duralumin structural members. This distributed the load throughout the aircraft, providing great redundancy in the event of damage. The first planes were delivered in July 1942. However, only 16 were used as bombers. By this time, four-engined heavy bombers such as the Handley Page Halifax and Short Stirling were in service. The Warwick was used for transport, anti-submarine reconnaissance and air-sea rescue instead. Using the bombsight and bomb release mechanism, they dropped lifeboats and supplies to downed aircrews.

Left: Three pictures showing the ground crew preparing and fitting the lifeboat to a Warwick ASR aircraft. It is interesting to see the amount of life-saving equipment packed into the boat (far left). It takes a number of men to position the boat under the belly of the aircraft (top right) and then to attach it securely (bottom right) ready for deployment.

In all, 712 Warwicks were built. They carried a crew of six and were armed with eight .303-inch Browning machine guns. The plane was 72 feet 3 inches long with a wingspan of 96 feet 8 inches. It had a top speed of 224mph, a range of 2,300 miles and a ceiling of 21,500 feet with a rate of climb of 660 feet a minute.

Right: A view of the forward section of an Avro Manchester Mark I of 207 Squadron, while running up the port-side Rolls-Royce Vulture II engine at Waddington, Lincolnshire. Easily visible in the nose are the bomb aimer's window, the forward gun turret and the pilot's cockpit.

Rolls-Royce Vulture Engine

The Rolls-Royce Vulture was a 24-cylinder X-block engine – that is, twinned V-block engines horizontally opposing each other. The Vulture was essentially two Rolls-Royce Peregrine V engines, which were supercharged Kestrel engines, joined at the crankcase. With a displacement of 44 litres it was designed to produce around 1,750 horsepower, but delivered only 1,450 to 1,550. It also suffered from frequent failures of the big-end connecting-rod bearings because of poor lubrication and problems with heat dissipation. These problems did not seem insuperable, but Rolls-Royce's smaller Merlin had already delivered the same power as the Vulture's original specification, so production was discontinued in 1941 after only 538 had been built.

The Vulture had been designed to go into the Hawker Tornado, which was cancelled in favour of the Typhoon, powered by the Napier Sabre. The Vulture-engined version of the Vickers Warwick bomber was also abandoned. The only plane to go into production using the Vulture was the twin-engined Avro Manchester.

The specification also made a series of other demands that were later abandoned. The plane should be able to act as a dive bomber, and also launch torpedoes and make catapult-assisted take-offs. Although these requirements were dropped, the result was that the Manchester – and later the Lancaster – was a very strong aircraft. One requirement that remained was that it should be able to carry a bomb load of 8,000lb, so Chadwick designed the Manchester around a very large single-celled bomb bay that took up some two-thirds of the length of the fuselage.

Avro received an order for 200 Manchesters on 1 July 1937, purely on the strength of the design. However, by 1938 it had become clear that the Rolls-Royce Vulture engine was not as powerful as expected – delivering only 1,450 to 1,550 of the promised 1,750 horsepower. Nor was it proving to be very reliable. Vickers Warwick developed their prototype using the Bristol Centaurus radial engine, then used the 1,850-horsepower American Pratt & Whitney Double Wasp in the production model. Handley Page dropped the Vulture from their prototype and instead installed four Merlin engines in the Halifax. Avro stuck with the Vulture.

Left: *Armourers prepare to load Avro Manchester Mark I, L7291, of 97 Squadron, with 1,000lb GP bombs at Coningsby, Lincolnshire, England.*

The first prototype of the Manchester flew at Manchester's Ringway Airport on 25 July 1939. This was very clearly the predecessor of the Lancaster; it had the distinctive twin-finned tailplane seen on the later aircraft. Although not installed in the first prototype, the design called for nose and tail turrets like those later seen on the Lancaster. Avro also began to make provision for a dorsal turret that appeared on the production models. The Mark I carried two .303-inch machine guns in the turret in the nose, two in the dorsal turret and four in the rear turret. Early Mark Is featured a belly or ventral turret, but this was dropped in favour of the dorsal turret.

Tests on the new aircraft revealed some problems. The wings had to be lengthened by nearly 10 feet, from a span of 80 feet 2 inches to one of 90 feet 1 inch. The aircraft also suffered from directional instability. This was reduced by adding a third tail-fin. This central fin appeared on the first 20 Manchester Mark Is. The main production model, the Mark IA, dropped this in favour of the twin tail with the enlarged, taller fin and rudders that were carried over to the Lancaster.

Above: An interior view of the Avro Manchester Mark I, L7288 EM-H, of 207 Squadron, looking aft towards the rear turret. A member of the crew is posing by the flare chute.

Right: The Manchester Mark IA, L7486, on an air test, shortly after delivery to 207 Squadron at Waddington, England. It carried the code letters EM-P and EM-Z during its service with the Squadron.

The Manchester went into service with 207 Squadron of RAF Bomber Command at RAF Waddington on 1 November 1940. It flew its first operational mission on 24 February 1941 in a raid against a German cruiser in the French port of Brest. For the Manchester, this was something of a success. None were lost and only one crashed on its return to base. However, by this time the Lancaster was already in the air and the Manchester's days were numbered.

By the time production finished in November 1941, Manchesters were in service with ten bomber squadrons and were being used by Coastal Command. Avro itself built 177 Manchesters, while Metropolitan-Vickers – formerly British Westinghouse – completed 32 aircraft under licence. The first 13 Metropolitan-Vickers made were destroyed in a German bombing raid on Trafford Park on 23 December 1941. Plans for Armstrong Whitworth and Fairey at Stockport to build the Manchester were abandoned. This was because Rolls-Royce had not overcome their problems with the Vulture engine. Rolls-Royce had more urgent jobs in 1939–40 than fixing the Vulture, and the entire project would soon be dropped.

Below: *The damaged tail section of Handley Page Halifax B Mark II, Series I, HR782 MH-V, of 51 Squadron, following its collision with an Avro Lancaster. They were returning from a raid on Munchen-Gladbach in Germany, on the night of 29/30 August 1943. HR782 was 10 miles from its temporary base at Ossington, Nottinghamshire, when the Lancaster, apparently on a reciprocal course, collided with the aircraft, damaging the port propellers, gashing the fuselage and tearing off the upper port fin. The pilot, Flying Officer R Burchett, found the aircraft uncontrollable at less than 180 mph, but made a good landing at Ossington despite overshooting the runway. HR782 was repaired and flew on further operations before it was finally lost on a raid to Leipzig on the night of 3/4 December 1943.*

The Manchester remained in squadron service until the end of June 1942. In all, 209 Manchesters were built before production switched to the Lancaster. Some 80 were lost in action, and another 50 to general unreliability; they were very vulnerable. Although their service ceiling was 19,200 feet, with a full bomb load the Manchester had to operate nearer 10,000 feet. In theory the Manchester could fly on one engine; the Vulture was so unreliable that it was often forced to do so. However, in practice it was impossible for a Manchester to cover any distance on one engine.

Despite its shortcomings, the Manchester did have some good features that were carried over to the Lancaster. The bomb bay was the biggest of any aircraft in Bomber Command at the time. This would allow the Lancaster to carry increasingly large bomb loads to Germany later in the war. Even the Manchester could manage the 4,000lb blockbuster bomb known as the 'Cookie'. The bomb aimer had a well-designed position under the front gun turret, with a good view through a perspex blister – another feature that was carried over to the Lancaster.

Almost as soon as the Manchester was airborne, work began on modifying it to use different engines. Both the Napier Sabre and Bristol Centaurus radial engines were tried in the prototype Manchester Mark II. However, none were put in production. It was then decided to use four of the less powerful, but much more reliable, Rolls-Royce Merlin engines in the Manchester Mark III. The prototype Mark III flew on 9 January 1941. Avro then managed to persuade the Air Ministry that switching to the four-Merlin version of the Manchester was preferable to retooling Avro's factories to make Handley Page Halifaxes. As the Manchester Mark III came off the production line, it was soon renamed the Avro Lancaster and would eventually become the primary weapon of Bomber Command.

Manchester Performance Statistics

Engines: Two Rolls-Royce Vultures

Horsepower: Theoretically 1,750hp (1,305kw), in practice 1,500hp (1,118kw)

Max speed: 265mph (426kmh) at 17,000 feet (5,181m)

Cruising speed: 185mph (298kmh) at 15,000 feet (4,522m)

Ceiling: 19,200 feet (5,852m), 10,000 feet (3,050m) with a full bomb load

Range: 1,630 miles (2,623 km) with 8,100lb (3,674kg) of bombs, 1,200 miles (1,931km) with 10,350lb (4,695kg) of bombs

Fuel capacity: 1,700 Imperial gallons (2,060.26 US gallons or 7,726 litres)

Span: 90 feet 1 inch (27.5m)

Length: 69 feet 4 inches (21.2m)

Bomb load: 10,350lb (4,695kg) of high-explosive bombs or incendiaries:

• 2x 18 inch (457mm) torpedoes, or

• 4x sea mines, or

• 4x 2,000lb (907kg) bombs, or

• 12x 500lb (227kg) bombs, or

• 2x 4,000lb (1,814kg) bombs, or

• 1x 4,000lb (1,814kg) bomb and 6 x 1,000lb (454kg) bombs

Front turret: FN5 turret with two 0.303 inch (7.7mm) Browning Mk II machine guns

Rear turret: FN20 turret with four 0.303 inch (7.7mm) Browning Mk II machine guns

Dorsal turret: FN7 or FN21A turret with two 0.303 inch (7.7mm) Browning Mk II machine guns.

Rolls-Royce Merlin

The Rolls-Royce Merlin was a liquid-cooled 27-litre V12 piston aircraft engine. Several versions of the Merlin were built by Rolls-Royce in Derby, Crewe and Glasgow, by Ford in Manchester and under licence by Packard in the United States. Originally developed as a fighter engine, it saw service in the Spitfire and the Hawker Hunter. Early Merlins were unreliable, but Rolls-Royce began taking random engines from the end of the assembly line and running them continuously at full power until they failed. They were then dismantled to find out which part had failed. That part was redesigned to be stronger. After two years of this programme, the Merlin had become one of the most reliable aeroplane engines in the world. It could be run at full power for 8-hour bombing missions without any problems.

The engine was continually upgraded. The Merlin II or III used in the Mark I Spitfire and Hurricane produced 1,030 horsepower. The Merlin XX fitted to Mark I Lancasters produced 1,280 horsepower. By the end of the war, they were delivering 1,620 horsepower.

Above: The first Aldershot prototype J6852, seen here in flight.

Avro Aldershot

The Avro Aldershot was Roy Chadwick's first attempt at designing a purpose-built bomber. It was designed to meet the British Air Ministry Specification 2/20 for an interim bomber. Two Aldershot I single-engined prototypes were produced; they first flew at Hamble Aerodrome in 1922. Afterwards the Rolls-Royce Condor engine was replaced with the water-cooled Napier Cub and the fuselage was lengthened by 6 feet. The converted prototypes became the Aldershot Mark II.

In 1923 the Air Ministry ordered 15 improved Aldershot Mark IIIs. On 1 April 1924, the first were sent to the newly formed 99 Squadron RAF, where they were used for night flying. However, the following year, the Air Ministry decided to use only multi-engined bombers and the Aldershots were replaced by the Handley Page Hyderabad.

The Aldershot carried a crew of three. It was 45 feet long, with a wingspan of 68 feet. It had a maximum speed of 110mph, a range of 625 miles and a ceiling of 14,500 feet. The plane could carry a 2,000lb load of bombs and had a Lewis gun in the rear cockpit for protection.

Below: This is an Aldershot III. The only operator of the aircraft was 99 Squadron, which was formed on 1 April 1924.

Left: A typical scene at RAF Mildenhall, as armourers of 149 Squadron fit bomb carriers to a pair of 1,000-pounders. In the background, Stirling N-Nuts runs up its engines.

Below: Short Stirling Mark I, W7429 LS-J, of 15 Squadron based at Wyton, Huntingdonshire, England, photographed while in flight from another aircraft of 15 Squadron.

Short Stirling

The Short Stirling was the first British four-engined bomber to fly. The prototype took to the air in May 1939. However, its undercarriage collapsed when it landed, and it was not until February 1941 that the aircraft made its first operational flight against the enemy.

Powered by four 1,375-horsepower Bristol Hercules radial engines, it was a sturdy and dependable aircraft. However, the specification limited its wingspan to under 100 feet so that it could fit into the standard RAF hangars of the day. Being later aircraft, the Lancaster and Halifax were allowed to exceed this. The wingspan of 99 feet 1 inch gave it a ceiling of just 16,500 feet. It could carry 1,800lb of bombs and was defended by eight 0.303 Browning machine guns – two in the nose turret, two in the dorsal turret and four in the tail turret.

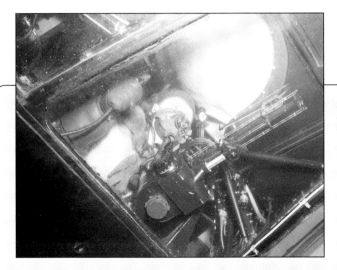

Left: *Close-up of a bomb aimer operating a Mark IXA Course-setting bombsight in the nose of a Short Stirling.*

In the autumn of 1943, the use of the Stirling in main force operations began to decline. A Bomber Command study of losses in raids on Nuremberg and Berlin between August and November of 1943 showed that between 10 and 15 per cent of the Stirlings were lost – a much higher percentage than either the Lancaster or Halifax. It was particularly vulnerable to the latest attacks from beneath of German night fighters fitted with upward-firing cannons. The Stirling was dropped from bombing operations early in 1944. However, it was still used for mine-laying, electronic countermeasures, transport, dropping agents and supplies, and pulling gliders.

Below: *Three Short Stirling aircraft in flight after taking off from an airbase in England.*

Left: The Lancaster prototype BT308, with its four Rolls-Royce Merlin X engines.

Chapter Five
Development of the Lancaster

T he Avro Lancaster was the most important British heavy bomber of World War II, and it became the mainstay of Bomber Command's aerial assault on Germany. It was the third of the four-engined heavy bombers to enter service. The first two were the Short Stirling and Handley Page Halifax, but the Lancaster soon overshadowed both of them.

This first prototype, BT308, shared three-quarters of its components with the Manchester, including, initially, the three-finned tailplane. However, the wingspan had to be extended from 90 feet to 100 feet to carry the four Rolls-Royce Merlin X engines. The plane was assembled by Avro's experimental flight department at Manchester's Ringway Airport where test pilot H A 'Bill' Thorn took the controls for its first flight on Thursday, 9 January 1941.

Right: Newly completed Avro Lancaster B Mark IIIs on the apron at the A V Roe Company factory at Woodford, Cheshire, England. NE124 (centre) served as OF-J with 97 Squadron, and was shot down over France by a German night fighter while raiding the flying-bomb site at Prouville, on the night of 24/25 June 1944. LM578 (second from right), a Yeadon-built example, served as EM-L with 207 Squadron RAF, with whom it crashed off the Dutch coast while outbound for a night raid on Wesseling, Germany, on 21/22 June 1944.

Left: A Lancaster Mk I of 83 Squadron in flight. The Mk I used the Rolls-Royce Merlin XX engines.

Tests with the prototype quickly showed that the new plane easily outperformed the Manchester. Improved engines and longer wings gave it a ceiling of over 20,000 feet and a range of over 2,000 miles. It could carry a bomb load of 14,000lb. This would later increase to 18,000lb. Orders were quickly placed for the new aircraft and Manchesters still on the Avro production line were converted.

A second prototype, DG595, saw three significant changes. The triple-finned tail of the early Manchester was replaced by the distinctive twin-finned Lancaster tail. The engines were changed to the Merlin XX, whose modified supercharger gave more power at higher altitudes. At first, four gun turrets were fitted – nose, tail, dorsal and ventral. However, the ventral turret never became standard on the Lancaster, although aircrews liked having a downward-firing gun.

Left: With so many men away fighting in the war – and flying Lancasters – women were employed to build the engines and the aircraft.

The first production aircraft, the Mark I, flew on 31 October 1941. It closely resembled the second prototype, and it is a tribute to the design that this remained the main version of the aircraft in flight until the end of World War II. The engine used was the 1,280-horsepower Merlin XX, which was later replaced by the Merlin 22 and then the more powerful Merlin 24.

Of the 7,737 Lancasters produced, 3,425 were Mark Is. However, another 3,469 were Mark IIIs or Mark Xs, which were essentially Mark Is powered by the American-produced Packard version of the Merlin engine. The four wing-mounted engines were fitted with three-bladed airscrews. It had a fixed tail-wheel and hydraulically operated main landing gear that retracted into the inner engine housing.

Right: *Since so many aircraft now used the Merlin engine, Rolls-Royce workers were kept busy turning out enough Merlins to keep the aircraft industry supplied.*

Left: *Shown here is a Lancaster B Mk X, which used four 1,280hp Rolls-Royce engines, manufactured by Packard in America.*

Above: *In August 1942, Lancaster I R5727 became the first of its type to fly the Atlantic, having been chosen as the pattern machine for production of the Lancaster in Canada. It is seen here at Prestwick Airport, Scotland, before the flight.*

Initially the Mark I had four Frazer-Nash turrets, armed with .303 Browning machine guns – two in the FN5 nose-mounted turret, two in the FN50 mid-upper turret, four in the FN20A tail turret and one in a FN64 ventral turret. This belly turret was phased out during 1942 after it proved to be of little use in action. This cut the Lancaster's crew to seven – a pilot, navigator, wireless operator, flight engineer, two gunners and the bomb aimer, who also manned the front gun turret.

The Lancaster's great advantage was that it could carry a heavy bomb load. What is more, its 33-foot bomb bay was undivided, so it could carry the increasingly large bombs used by Bomber Command during the war. The standard Lancaster Mark I was able to carry the 12,000lb Tallboy bomb, introduced in 1944, within the bay. However, the bomb-bay doors had to be adapted. Armour plating and even some defensive armament had to be removed in an attempt to get the Lancaster up to the height required for the Tallboy to be effective.

More armaments and the bomb-bay doors had to be removed so the Lancaster could carry the 22,000lb Grand Slam 'earthquake' bombs. Merlin 24 engines had to be used for their better take-off performance. Otherwise, the plane was little different from the Lancasters that were rolling off the production line at the end of 1941.

Based at RAF Waddington near Lincoln, 44 Squadron received its first delivery of the production model on 24 December 1941. The squadron had had the first prototype Lancaster since 9 September 1941 to familiarize themselves with it, and had been using the Manchester, so it was easy for the aircrew to make the changeover. The squadron mounted its first operation using Lancasters on 3 March 1942. This was a so-called 'gardening' mission, laying mines off the German coast close to Heligoland. All four Lancasters used in the operation returned safely. The Lancaster made its first attack on Germany on 10 March, when two joined a raid on Essen. By this time 97 Squadron had also received its Lancasters, making its first raid on 20 March.

Above: A group of Lancaster IIIs flying high through the skies over England. Each of these aircraft used four Packard-built Merlin 28 engines.

Below: Three Avro Lancaster B Mark Is of 44 Squadron, based at Waddington, Lincolnshire, England, flying above the clouds. Left to right: W4125, KM-W, being flown by Sergeant Colin Watt, Royal Australian Air Force; W4162, KM-Y, flown by Pilot Officer T G Hackney (later killed while serving with 83 Squadron); and W4187, KM-S, flown by Pilot Officer J D V S Stephens DFM, who was killed with his crew two nights later during a raid on Wismar, Germany.

Lancaster

Crew: 7

Length: 69 feet 5 inches (21.18m)

Wingspan: 102 feet (31.09m)

Height: 19 feet 7 inches (5.97m)

Wing area: 1,300 square feet (120m²)

Empty weight: 36,828lb (16,705kg)

Loaded weight: 63,000lb (28,580kg)

Powerplant: 4x Rolls-Royce Merlin XX V12 engines, 1,280 horsepower (954kW) each

Performance

Maximum speed: 240 knots (280mph, 450kmh) at 15,000ft (5,600m)

Range: 2,700 nm (3,000mi, 4,600km) with minimal bomb load

Service ceiling: 23,500 feet (8,160m)

Wing loading: 48lb per square foot (240kg/m²)

Power/mass: 0.082 horsepower per lb (130W/kg)

Armament

Guns: 8x 0.303 inch (7.70mm) Browning machine guns in three turrets, with variations

Bombs: maximum – 22,000lb (9,980kg)
typical – 14,000lb (6,350kg)

Handley Page Halifax

Crew: 7

Length: 71 feet 7 inches (21.82m)

Wingspan: 104 feet 2 inches (31.75m)

Height: 20 feet 9 inches (6.32m)

Wing area: 1,190 square feet (110.6m²)

Loaded weight: 54,400lb (24,675kg)

Powerplant: 4x Bristol Hercules XVI radial engines, 1,615 horsepower (1,205kW) each

Performance

Maximum speed: 282mph (454kmh) at 13,500 feet (4,115m)

Range: 1,860mi (3,000km) combat

Service ceiling: 24,000 feet (7,315m)

Rate of climb: 750 feet a minute (3.8m/s)

Wing loading: 45.7lb per square foot (223.1kg/m²)

Power/mass: 0.12 horsepower per lb (195W/kg)

Armament

Guns: 8x .303 inch (7.7mm) Browning machine guns (4 in dorsal turret, 4 in tail turret), 1x .303 inch (7.7mm) Vickers K machine gun in nose

Bombs: 13,000lb (5,897kg)

Junkers JU 390

Crew: 10

Length: 112 feet 2 inches (34.20m)

Wingspan: 165 feet 1 inch (50.30m)

Height: 22 feet 7 inches (6.89m)

Wing area: 2,730 square feet (254m²)

Empty weight: 87,100lb (39,508kg)

Loaded weight: 117,092lb (53,112kg)

Max take-off weight: 166,449lb (75,500kg)

Powerplant: 6x BMW 801D radial engines, 1,730 horsepower (1,272kW) each

Performance

Maximum speed: 314mph (505kmh)

Range: 6,030mi (9,700km)

Service ceiling: 19,700 feet (6,000m)

Wing loading: 42.8lb per square foot (209kg/m²)

Power/mass: 0.10 horsepower per lb (0.17W/kg)

Armament

Guns: 2x 20mm MG 151/20 cannons in dorsal turrets, 1x 20mm MG 151/20 in tail, 2x 13mm MG 131 machine guns at waist, 2x 13mm MG 131 in gondola

Bombs: 3,968 lb (1,800kg)

Boeing B-29 Superfortress

Crew: 11

Length: 99 feet 0 inches (30.2m)

Wingspan: 141 feet 3 inches (43.1m)

Height: 29 feet 7 inches (8.5m)

Wing area: 1,736 square feet (161.3m^2)

Empty weight: 74,500lb (33,793kg)

Loaded weight: 120,000lb (54,431kg)

Max take-off weight: 133,500lb (60,554kg)

Powerplant: 4x Wright R-3350-23 and 23A turbosupercharged radial engines, 2,200 horsepower (1,640kW) each

Performance

Maximum speed: 357mph (310 knots, 574kmh)

Cruise speed: 220mph (190 knots, 350kmh)

Stall speed: 105mph (91 knots, 170kmh)

Combat range: 3,250mi (2,820nm, 5,230km)

Ferry range: 5,600mi (4,900nm, 9,000km)

Service ceiling: 33,600 feet (10,200m)

Rate of climb: 900 feet a minute (4.6m/s)

Wing loading: 69.12lb square foot (337kg/m^2)

Power/mass: 0.073 horsepower per lb (121W/kg)

Armament

Guns: 8 to 10x .50 inch (12.7mm) calibre Browning M2/ANs in remote controlled turrets, 2 x .50 inch and 1x 20mm M2 cannon in tail position (the cannon was eventually removed as it proved unreliable in service)

Bombs: 20,000lb (9,000kg) standard; modified to carry two 22,000lb (10,000kg) T-14 'earthquake' bombs externally

Right: Avro Lancaster bombers nearing completion at the A V Roe factory in Woodford, Cheshire, England.

Chapter Six

Construction

The Lancaster bomber is a mid-wing cantilevered monoplane with an oval all-metal fuselage. Both the wings and fuselage were made in five sections. They were built separately, then fitted with all the equipment required before being brought together for final assembly. The tail unit with its twin oval fins and rudders could also be made separately. This meant that the production could be dispersed around a number of different factories, which had obvious advantages in wartime when production facilities risked coming under air attack.

Of the 7,737 Lancasters, nearly half were built at Avro's factories at Woodford and Chadderton in Manchester. They were test-flown from Woodford Aerodrome in Cheshire. Some 1,080 Lancasters were also built by Metropolitan-Vickers in Manchester and tested at Woodford. Another 700 Lancasters were built at a 'shadow' factory next to Yeadon Aerodrome, now Leeds Bradford Airport, northwest Leeds. The factory employed some 17,500 workers at a time when the population of Yeadon was just 10,000. The old taxiway from the factory to the runway is still visible. Other Lancasters were made by Armstrong Whitworth. The test pilot at Castle Bromwich, Alex Henshaw – who is said to have test-flown 10 per cent of all Spitfires – is the only pilot known to have barrel-rolled a Lancaster bomber.

Right: An aerial view of the Chadderton factory taken in the 1960s.

Above: Avro Lancaster aircraft under construction at the Avro factory at Woodford, Cheshire.

This was considered almost impossible because of the slow speed of the plane. Later in the war, Lancasters were made at the Austin Motor Company works in Longbridge, Birmingham. Then after the war, they were made by Vickers-Armstrong at Chester. The Lancaster Mark X variant was manufactured by Victory Aircraft in Malton, Ontario. Some 430 were built, using Packard-built Merlin engines and American-style instrumentation and electrics.

The planes were not cheap to make. In 1943 it cost between £45,000 and £50,000 to build a Lancaster; this would be equivalent to £1.5 to £1.6 million in 2008.

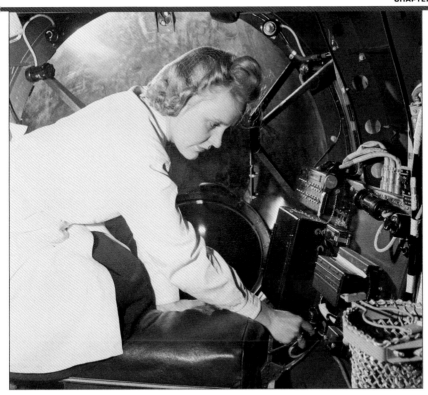

Left: A female electrical worker, fitting the bomb aimer's switch into the half-completed fuselage of an Avro Lancaster, in a factory in the north of England.

Left: The crew of the first Canadian-built Lancaster X to arrive in Britain, KB700, christened the 'Ruhr Express', photographed with their mascot at Northolt, Middlesex, on 15 September 1943. They are, left to right: Squadron Leader Reg Lane DSO, DFC (pilot), Pilot Officer Johnny Carrere (navigator), Sergeant Ross Webb (WOP/AG), Flight Sergeant Reg Burgar (mid-upper gunner) with 'Bambi', Pilot Officer Steve Boczar (co-pilot), Flight Sergeant R Wright DFM (bomb aimer) and Sergeant Mike Baczinski (flight engineer).

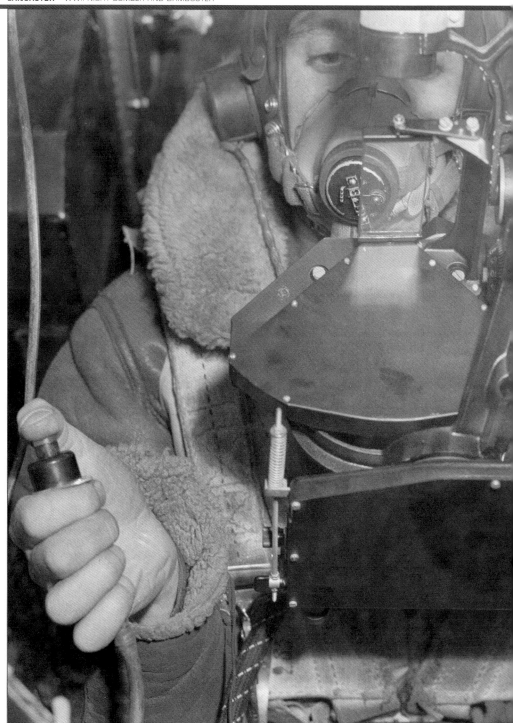

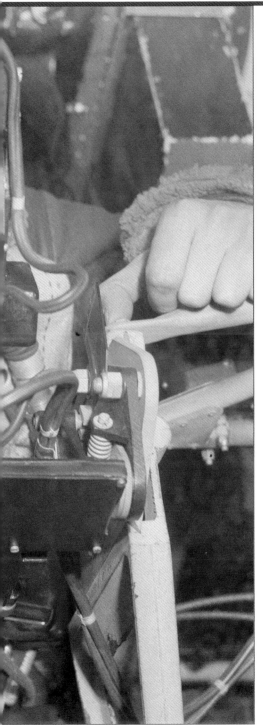

Left: The bomb aimer on board an Avro Lancaster B Mark III of 619 Squadron, operating a Mark XIV Stabilized Vector Bombsight at his position in the nose of the aircraft.

The conditions for the crew were not comfortable. It was cramped and very noisy – crew members communicated by wireless. The planes were unpressurized and crewmen had oxygen masks. There was no heating in the plane, which meant that at altitude it was very cold. It soon became clear that heating of the guns and turrets was necessary in order to maintain the efficiency of both guns and gunners, who plugged in electrically heated suits to prevent frostbite and hypothermia. However, it was not until 1944 that gun heaters became generally available. This did not help the rear gunners, because they usually insisted on having nearly all the perspex removed from the turret to give a completely unobstructed view. The Lancaster also had little spare electrical capacity to power the gun heaters. Eventually ducts were added to channel heat from the engines to the dorsal and rear turrets. This began in August 1944 and, by the end of the war, around half the Lancasters had heating ducts fitted.

The bomb aimer was particularly uncomfortable. He had to lie prone on the floor in the nose of the aircraft, looking out of the large transparent perspex nose cone. The controls for the bombsight were in front of him. To his right were the bomb release selectors; to his left the bombsight computer. This was a mechanical system. The bomb aimer fed in the wind speed, direction and altitude, and the machine calculated the accurate release of bombs from a moving aircraft.

The bomb aimer usually doubled as the forward gunner. To man the FN5 nose turret, he simply had to stand up. Then he would be in position behind the twin Browning .303 machine guns. When he was not aiming bombs or manning the nose gun, he would be looking out of the nose cupola to assist the navigator. He was also in the easiest position to escape if the plane was hit. The bomb aimer's position had a parachute exit in the floor. The drawback was that it was forward of the engines.

Bombsights

Early Lancasters used the Mark IX Course-Setting Bombsight. This was a preset vector bombsight, where ground speed and drift angle were computed from assumed wind and airspeed. It had to be set manually, based on aircraft speed, altitude and bomb load. The bomb aimer then had to squint through its wires. It would have to be adjusted manually if any of the parameters changed, and in 1942 it was replaced by the Mark XIV, also known as the Blackett bombsight.

Invented by Cambridge physicist Patrick Blackett, the Mark XIV was another vector bombsight where the bomb aimer entered various details of the bomb load, target altitude and wind direction. An analogue computer then calculated the trajectory of the bombs and projected an inverted sword shape onto the glass of the sight. When the target was at the intersection, the bombs were released. The advantage was that the plane did not have to make a level bombing run beforehand.

After the Blackett bombsight proved itself in action, manufacture was moved to the United States, where it was re-engineered to American standards. Electric gyros were added and it became the T1. Precision raids used a Stabilizing Automatic Bombsight, or SABS, which again used a gyroscopically stabilized platform. However, corrections could also be made for temperature and wind speed.

Below: A view into the bomb aimer's bubble, showing his position. The equipment on the left, with a green bar around it, is the bomb computer and the yellow line seen on the floor goes around the front escape hatch. The small switches on the right are the bomb selector switches and the piece below that is the timing mechanism for the release of the bombs. The Mk XIV bombsight (left) was generally used for area bombing and introduced into operational service by the RAF in 1942. It was also known as the Blackett bombsight, after the man who invented it – Patrick Blackett.

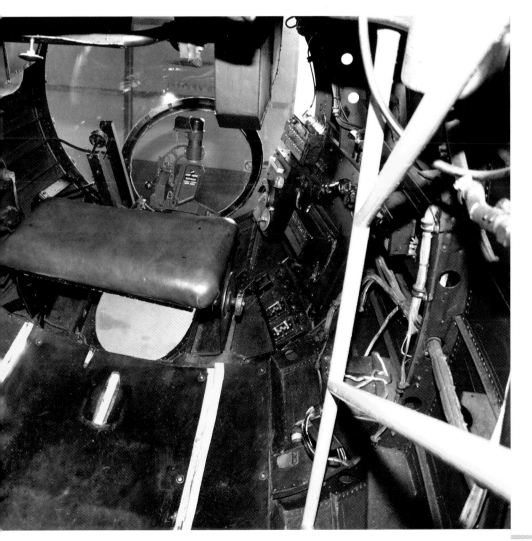

Left: The pilot of an Avro Lancaster of 103 Squadron, based at Elsham Wolds, Lincolnshire, wearing his oxygen mask while flying the aircraft at high altitude.

Below: The instrumentation and controls from the pilot's point of view.

The pilot and flight engineer sat side-by-side on the roof of the bomb bay. Above them was the expansive canopy which gave good visibility above and to the front and sides. The pilot sat to the left on a raised portion of the floor. The flight engineer sat to the right of the pilot on a collapsible seat, known as a dicky seat. The fuel gauges and controls were on a panel behind him and to his right.

Below: The flight engineer on board an Avro Lancaster B Mark III of 619 Squadron, based at Coningsby, Lincolnshire, checks settings on the control panel from his seat in the cockpit. His seat would fold out from the side of the cockpit wall so that he could be positioned next to the pilot.

Directly behind them sat the navigator. He was screened off by a curtain so the light he worked by did not show in the night sky. There was a large chart table in front of him. Above it was an instrument panel showing altitude, airspeed, direction of flight and other information he needed for navigation. Aft of the chart table were the radios. Most British-built Lancasters were fitted with the R1155 receiver and T1154 transmitter, while the Canadian-built aircraft and those built for service in the Far East had American radios. These provided radio direction-finding, as well as voice- and Morse code transmission.

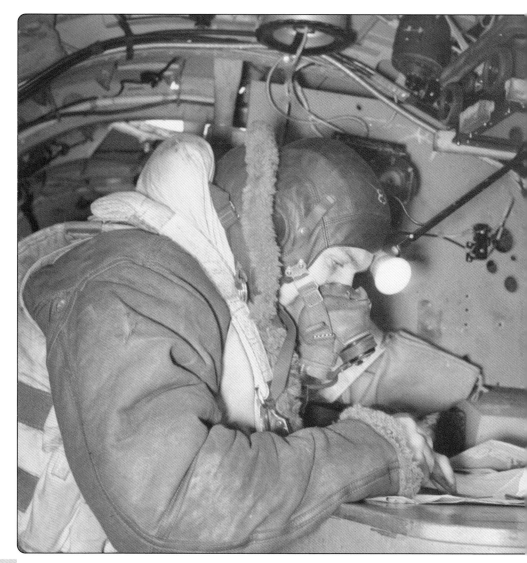

Navigational Aids

In March 1942 the GEE radio navigational system was introduced. Stations in Britain transmitted pulsed signals. From the intervals between the pulses when the signal was received on board, it was possible to work out where the plane was, usually to within around a mile over western Germany or within 2 miles at the extreme range. This was not a beamed system like the one the Germans used, by which the defenders could work out the direction of attack and likely target.

The more accurate Oboe system was introduced in December 1942. It used a radio transponder that picked up signals from two stations transmitting from widely separated locations in southern England. One radar beam pointed in the direction of the target, while the other tracked the Oboe-equipped bomber. The operator in the control station could guide the aircraft directly on to the target. However, the system could only direct one aircraft at a time, so it was fitted to the Pathfinder aircraft that led the main force of Lancasters on to the target. Later, the GEE-H 'blind bombing' system was introduced, which could handle up to 80 planes at a time. Aircraft fitted with the GEE-H system were usually marked with two horizontal yellow stripes on the fins.

Some Lancasters were fitted with Automatic Gun-Laying Turrets in 1944. Codenamed Village Inn, they used radar to plot the target so that it could be tracked and fired upon in total darkness.

Left: *The navigator of an Avro Lancaster B Mark III of 619 Squadron based at Coningsby, Lincolnshire, seated at his table in the aircraft.*

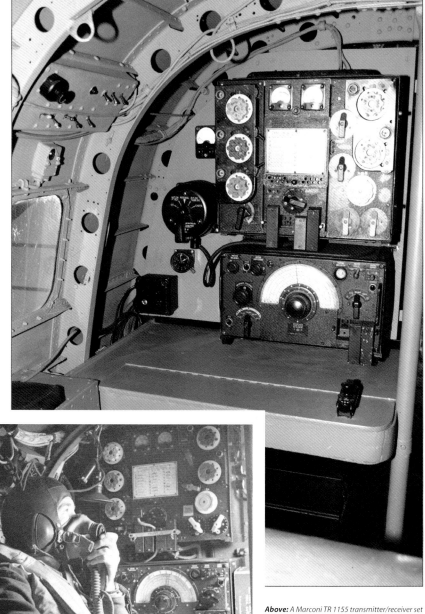

Above: *A Marconi TR 1155 transmitter/receiver set as fitted to the Lancaster 'Just Jane' – now preserved at the Lincolnshire Aviation Heritage Museum, England. A wireless operator (left) on board an Avro Lancaster B Mark I of 57 Squadron based at Scampton, Lincolnshire, speaking to the pilot from his position in front of the Marconi TR 1154/55 transmitter/receiver set.*

Left: The rear gunner of an Avro Lancaster of 630 Squadron, based at East Kirkby, Lincolnshire, checks his guns in the Nash and Thompson FN20 tail turret, before taking off for a night raid on the marshalling yards at Juvisy-sur-Orge, France.

Right: Always a lonely and very dangerous post, this is a view into the seating position of the rear gunner.

The wireless operator sat behind them on the main spar, facing forward. To his left was a window, and above him there was a transparent dome that he could use to make visual signals to other planes or to ground crew when they were on the ground. The navigator could also use the dome to see the stars for celestial navigation.

Beyond the wireless operator were the two wing spars. These created a major obstacle for crew members moving up and down the fuselage even when the plane was on the ground. Further down the fuselage, the floor dropped as it passed beyond the bomb bay. The mid-upper gunner sat there on a piece of canvas slung under the FN50 dorsal turret. The perspex turret gave him a 360-degree view over the top of the aircraft. His two Browning .303 machine guns protected the plane against attacks above and to the side. For him, it was an uncomfortable ride, as he would often have to occupy his canvas seat for up to 8 hours at a time.

Behind the dorsal turret on the starboard side was the side crew door. This was the main entrance to the aircraft and could also be used as a parachute exit. Beyond the spars supporting the tailplane sat the rear gunner in the FN20, FN120 or Rose Rice turret. In the FN20 and FN120 turrets he had four Browning .303 machine guns. The Rose Rice had two .50 Brownings. Of all the crewmen, the rear gunner was the most exposed to enemy fire and the mortality rate for rear gunners was extremely high.

Below: Lancaster B Mark III, JB743 CF-C Captain, of 625 Squadron, based at Kelstern, Lincolnshire, taxiing in at Mount Farm, Oxfordshire. Note the 'Monica' tail-warning radar aerial beneath the rear turret. JB743 was lost during a raid by No1 Group on the railway yards at Vierzon on the night of 30 June/1 July, 1944.

Later developments changed the appearance of the Lancaster. In 1943 the downward-looking H2S radar was introduced. This was a navigational aid that could identify large bodies of water and built-up areas, vital when carrying out area bombing. The aerials of the H2S were housed in a pear-shaped radome underneath the rear fuselage. A more short-lived addition was a rearward-looking radar called Monica. This was designed to detect incoming night fighters, but was abandoned after it was discovered that the Germans were homing in on its radar signals.

Top Right: Wellington Mark II, Z8524 U, of 104 Squadron, about to be loaded with 500lb GP bombs, for a sortie on a landing ground in North Africa. The front turret has been removed from this aircraft, which also carries 52 operation symbols on its nose.

Radar Equipment

In early 1943, Lancasters were fitted with the H2S downward-looking radar system which could identify built-up areas for night-time and all-weather bombing raids. However, this had to be used with discretion, as German night fighters were fitted with the Naxos receiver that could detect its signal, allowing them to home in on the aircraft. Later, the Fishpond system was added under the Lancaster. This detected fast-moving German night fighters within 30 miles and displayed their position on a second screen.

In the spring of 1942, the rearward-looking Monica radar system was introduced. It warned of the approach of night fighters. However, early in 1944, Germany equipped its fighters with the Flensburg receiver which used the Monica radar as a homing beacon. However, on the morning of 13 July 1944, a Junkers Ju 88G-1 night fighter equipped with a Flensburg receiver landed by mistake at RAF Woodbridge. After examining the equipment, Bomber Command removed Monica from their planes.

The Boozer radar detection system was also added to the Lancaster. A system of lights on the aircraft's instrument panel would light up if the plane was being tracked by German Würzburg ground radar or the Lichtenstein airborne radar. It proved not to be very useful, as pilots were plagued with false alarms. The airspace above Germany was full of radar signals that would trigger the detector.

Right: Halifax Mark II Series 1, L9619 ZA-E, of 10 Squadron based at Leeming, Yorkshire, England, in flight. This aircraft is an early production model fitted with beam gun hatches amidships instead of a mid-upper turret.

Vickers Wellington

More Wellingtons took to the air in World War II than any other British bomber. It was the only British bomber to serve in that role from 1939 until 1945, and remained in frontline service with Bomber Command until 1943.

The Wellington was designed by Neville Barnes Wallis, who developed the geodetic method of aircraft production. The fuselage was made of a lightweight grid of relatively simple parts, giving a 'basket weave' structure that was covered with a layer of cloth. The first aircraft produced for the RAF using this system was the Vickers Wellesley, a single-engined bomber that entered service in 1937.

The Wellington was designed to Air Ministry B.9/32 Bomber Specification, which called for a daylight twin-engined bomber with a range of 720 miles capable of carrying a 1,000lb bomb load. During its development, the performance increased. When the first prototype flew on 15 June 1936, it was capable of carrying 4,500lb in bombs, and had a maximum range of 1,800 miles. After an initial order for 180 Wellingtons was placed, the design was changed again. The Wellington was now to be a night bomber, with three powered gun turrets, including a retractable ventral turret under the bomber. The fuselage was also redesigned, making it taller, with more interior space.

The first Mark I Wellington flew on 23 December 1937. This was the first of 11,461 Wellingtons that would serve in Europe, the Mediterranean, North Africa and the Far East. Once equipped with self-sealing fuel tanks, the Wellington proved to be a very robust aircraft, capable of taking an amazing amount of damage thanks to its geodetic construction.

The Wellington carried a crew of six. It was 64 feet 7 inches long with a wingspan of 86 feet 2 inches. Its two 1,050-horsepower Bristol Pegasus radial engines gave it a top speed of 235mph and a climb rate of 1,050 feet per minute. It carried eight .303 inch Browning machine guns, two each in the nose and tail turrets, and two either side of the waist of the aircraft.

Handley Page Halifax

Alongside the Avro Lancaster, the Halifax brought the war home to Germany during the great bombing raids of 1944. Both were originally designed as twin-engined bombers using the Rolls-Royce Vulture engine. After the failure of this engine, both were forced to adapt their design to use four Merlin engines.

Work on the new prototype began early in 1938. It took to the air on 25 October 1939. A fully armed prototype first flew on 18 August 1940. Two months later the first production plane was airborne.

Like the Lancaster, the Halifax had been designed to be produced in parts. At its peak, there were six production lines, with some 41 companies in the Halifax Group involved in its production. In all 6,174 Halifax bombers were produced. The second most important plane in Bomber Command, the Halifax dropped over 200,000 tons of bombs during World War II.

Left: Air Marshal Sir Arthur 'Bomber' Harris, Commander-in-Chief of Royal Air Force Bomber Command, seated at his desk at Bomber Command Headquarters, High Wycombe, Buckinghamshire.

Chapter Seven

The Fighting Plane

❝ *The Nazis entered this war under the rather childish delusion that they were going to bomb everyone else, and nobody was going to bomb them* **❞**

commented Air Marshal Sir Arthur 'Bomber' Harris, who was appointed as head of Bomber Command in February 1942.

❝ *At Rotterdam, London, Warsaw and half a hundred other places, they put their rather naive theory into operation. They sowed the wind, and now they are going to reap the whirlwind.* **❞**

With the Lancaster, Harris had the tool to do the job. Now he had a high-altitude bomber that could drop large quantities of bombs on German cities.

During the early years of the war, the RAF had restricted themselves to the precision bombing of military and industrial targets while the Luftwaffe blitzed British cities. However, in 1942 this would change, and Bomber Command began the terror-bombing of German cities.

Below: The devastation caused in British cities during the Blitz was beyond most people's comprehension. Air war was new. Although the emergency services were always on high-alert, they were overwhelmed with the destruction the German bombers inflicted. Other cities around Europe were treated to the same by Hitler's Luftwaffe, but soon the tables would turn and it would be the Lancaster that would take revenge on the cities of Germany.

Left: *Armourers make final checks on the bomb load of an Avro Lancaster B Mark I of 207 Squadron at Syerston, Nottinghamshire, before a night bombing operation to Bremen, Germany. The mixed load (Bomber Command executive codeword 'Usual') consists of a 4,000lb HC bomb ('Cookie') and small bomb containers (SBCs) filled with 30lb incendiaries, with the addition of four 250lb target indicators (TI).*

Opposite: *Inside an empty bomb bay (left), showing the clamps and fitments that hold the assorted bombs. The huge doors at either side close to hide the deadly package.*

The policy changed due to analysis of aerial photographs from the early raids. They showed that less than one-third of bombs dropped by Bomber Command during the first two years of the war fell within 5 miles of the intended target. Indeed, due to equipment failure, enemy action, weather, or simply getting lost, only about 5 per cent of the planes that set out got within 5 miles of their target. As a result, there were plans to transfer the RAF's resources to the Army and Navy.

RAF commanders responded with a report of their own. It analyzed the damage inflicted on British cities by the Blitz and concluded that a bomber force of 4,000 planes could destroy the 43 German towns with a population of more than 100,000. They believed that this would weaken Germany sufficiently to allow the British Army to land back on continental Europe. Consequently, the strategy was changed. On 14 February 1942, the Air Ministry issued the Area Bombing Directive authorizing Bomber Command to attack "without restriction" primary targets that included Essen, Duisburg, Düsseldorf and Cologne, and secondary targets that included Braunschweig, Lübeck, Rostock, Bremen, Kiel, Hanover, Frankfurt, Mannheim, Stuttgart and Schweinfurt. Operations were to destroy the "morale of the enemy civilian population and in particular, the industrial workers". Liddell Hart's theory was about to be put into practice.

Eight days after the directive was issued, Air Marshal Arthur Harris – known universally as 'Bomber' Harris – was appointed commander of Bomber Command. His aim was to make German cities physically uninhabitable and make German civilians ever conscious that they were in personal danger. He was soon organizing 1,000-bomber raids, and the Lancaster would be in the front line.

An important feature of the Lancaster was its huge 33-foot bomb bay. This meant that a bombing force would rain down thousands of tons of high explosives and incendiaries on a built-up area. The aim was to create a firestorm that would burn out of control, destroying more of the city than the original bombing. Initially, the heaviest bombs carried were 4,000lb blockbuster bombs known as 'cookies'. Bulged bomb-bay doors were fitted subsequently, allowing the Lancaster to carry 8,000lb and, later, 12,000lb high-capacity bombs. These had thin casings so that around three-quarters of their weight was explosive. In normal, medium-capacity bombs, only half the weight was explosive, and the rest was bomb casing that caused damage when it fragmented.

Left: A still from film shot in an Avro Lancaster, by the RAF Film Production Unit, during a daylight attack on the Luftwaffe airfield and signals depot at St Cyr, France, by aircraft of No 5 Group. A 4,000lb HC bomb ('Cookie') and a smaller 500lb MC bomb can be seen just after they were released over the target. (Bottom left) This is a 500lb bomb, small when compared to the larger 2,000 and 4,000lb bombs. Many would accompany the larger bombs.

Below: A still shot by the RAF Film Production Unit during 'Operation Hurricane'. An Avro Lancaster B Mark I, NG128 SR-B, of 101 Squadron, piloted by Warrant Officer R B Tibbs, releases a 4,000lb HC bomb ('cookie') and 30lb incendiary bombs over the target during a special daylight raid on Duisburg. Over 2,000 sorties were dispatched to the city during 14–15 October 1944, in order to demonstrate Bomber Command's overwhelming superiority in German skies. Note also the large aerials on top of the Lancaster's fuselage, indicating that the aircraft is carrying 'Airborne Cigar' (ABC), a jamming device which disrupted enemy radio telephone channels.

The high-capacity – or HC – bombs were merely a drum full of explosives. They did not have fins and were in no way aerodynamic, but accuracy was not important. They were designed to blow the tiles off roofs so that the smaller 4lb incendiary bombs could fall inside, setting buildings on fire.

The 4,000lb cookie was 2 feet 6 inches in diameter and could be carried by Wellington bombers, as well as the Mosquitoes of the Light Night Strike Force. Later they became part of the standard bomb load of the RAF's heavy night bombers. The 4,000lb cookie was considered particularly dangerous to carry. Even if they jettisoned unarmed, the airflow over the detonation pistols fitted in the nose would often cause them to explode.

The cookie was usually dropped in a mixed load with smaller, aerodynamically shaped, bombs. Over the target, it was important to release the aerodynamically shaped bombs first. If the cookie was dropped first, the aerodynamically shaped bombs would catch up with it and could collide, blowing up the bombs and, possibly, the aircraft in mid-air.

Gradually the cookies got larger. The 8,000lb version was made from two 4,000lb sections, 3 feet 2 inches in diameter. A 12,000lb version was created by adding a third 4,000lb section. The 8,000lb cookie could only be carried by the Handley Page Halifax and the Lancaster; the 12,000lb version only by the Lancaster.

A Lancaster bomber would carry up to 14 Small Bomb Containers. Each container carried 236 4lb or 24 30lb incendiary bombs. This meant that each Lancaster could drop up to 3,304 4lb or 336 30lb incendiaries over a target. However, a Lancaster would usually carry one 4,000lb high-explosive cookie plus 12 Small Bomb Containers. With the cookie blowing the roof off and the incendiaries falling inside, this destructive mixture would set whole areas of a city on fire, sometimes creating unstoppable fire storms. The Lancaster also dropped conventional 1,000lb bombs. They dropped no fewer than 217,640 between 1942 and 1945.

The Lancaster was, of course, selected to deliver the bouncing bombs to the Ruhr dams in 1943. Then, in 1944, Barnes Wallis produced his first large bomb, the Tallboy. He had come up with the idea in 1941, but had put it aside when the Victory bomber was shelved. The Lancaster was the only plane that could carry the 21-foot-long Tallboy which, like the 8,000lb cookie, was 3 feet 2 inches in diameter. Even then, the plane had to be substantially modified.

Above: If you take a visit to the Battle of Britain Memorial Flight visitor centre, Coningsby, Lincolnshire, you will see this bomb as you approach the centre. This is an example of a Tallboy bomb, which was designed by Barnes Wallis, who also designed the 'bouncing bomb' for the 'Dambusters' raid. The Tallboy weighed 12,000lb (over 5 tons). It was designed to be dropped near to its target, where it would penetrate the ground, nose first, before causing a massive underground explosion. The earthquake effect would then cause the target structure to collapse.

Left: A 12,000lb MC deep-penetration bomb (Bomber Command Executive codeword 'Tallboy') is hoisted from the bomb dump to its carrier at Woodhall Spa, Lincolnshire, to be loaded into an Avro Lancaster of 617 Squadron. This would be used for a raid on the V-weapon site at Wizernes, France. 617 Squadron were unable to bomb the target on this occasion because of low cloud cover, but were to succeed two days later.

The Tallboy was the antithesis of the HC bomb. Of its 12,000lb, only 5,200lb were explosives. The rest was high-tensile steel casing so, when dropped from a great height, it would penetrate concrete or earth to a great depth without breaking apart. It was also given an aerodynamic shape so that it could reach a much higher velocity to increase its penetration. It also had tail fins that were given a slight twist. Early designs tended to tumble, but the twist of the fin made the bomb spin. The gyroscopic effect kept the nose pointing down, improving the aerodynamics and the accuracy. The bomb would actually pass through the sound barrier as it fell so, like the German V-2 rocket, the sound of the weapon falling would be heard after the explosion.

When it was dropped from 20,000 feet, the Tallboy reached a terminal velocity of around 2,500mph, or 3,666 feet per second – sound travels around 1,000 feet per second. The Tallboy had the penetrating power of an armour-piercing bomb, coupled with the explosive force of a large high-capacity blast bomb. It could penetrate 16 feet of concrete or displace 5,000 tons of earth, leaving a crater 80 feet deep and 100 feet wide.

To reach anything like the altitude required, the Lancaster had to be specially adapted. The armour plating and even defensive armaments were stripped out to reduce weight. The bomb-bay doors also had to be adapted to cope with the length of the bomb. Even then the Lancaster could only reach around 25,000 feet carrying a Tallboy, not the 40,000 feet Wallis had hoped for.

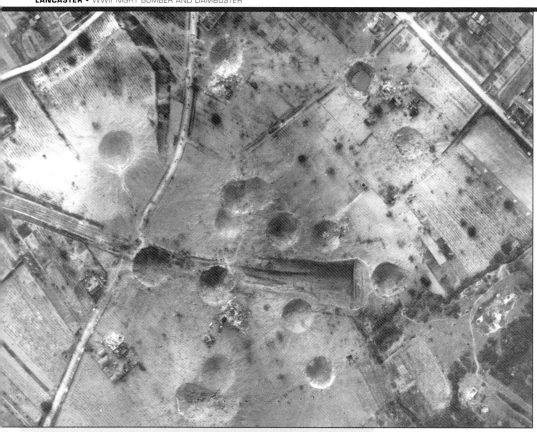

Above: Aerial reconnaissance photo, taken from 10,000 feet, showing the southern entrance of the Saumur railway tunnel following the attack on it by 22 Avro Lancasters of 617 Squadron on the night of 8/9 June 1944. This raid was the first occasion on which the 12,000lb 'Tallboy' deep-penetration bomb was used operationally. The target was marked by the Squadron Commander, Wing Commander G L Cheshire, who delivered his spotfires from an altitude of 500 feet, and the accuracy of the subsequent bombing, delivered between 8,000 and 11,000 feet, is attested by the 18 craters which can be counted within 220 yards of the tunnel mouth. One 'Tallboy' has pierced the roof of the tunnel, and there are two further direct hits on the railway tracks 100 yards from the entrance. The tunnel was blocked for a considerable period and, consequently, the movement of a German tank unit to the Normandy battlefront was badly delayed.

Precision was also important, and 617 'Dambusters' Squadron, who dropped the Tallboy, were trained in the use of the new Stabilizing Automatic Bombsight.

The bomb was filled with Torpex, which is 50 per cent more explosive than TNT by weight. It had three fuses in case one or two were knocked out on impact. The fuses were set to detonate between 30 seconds and 30 minutes after the bomb hit, to give it time to penetrate the target.

Below: A 12,000lb MC bomb ('Tallboy'), seen immediately after its release
from Avro Lancaster B Mark I, JB139, of 617 Squadron over the flying-bomb
store at Watten, France.

While Tallboy proved capable of penetrating even hardened reinforced concrete to devastating effect, this was not Barnes Wallis's intention. He had not designed the bomb to hit the target at all. Instead it was supposed to land close to it and penetrate the soil or rock the structure was built on. Then, when it exploded, the blast would shake the building to pieces, or create an underground cavern or camouflet that it fell into. This earthquake effect would cause more damage than a direct hit, where the blast would be contained to some extent by the structure of the building.

Tallboys were precision-built. They were essentially handmade, and their construction was labour-intensive. Consequently, if they were not used on a raid because the plane could not find or identify the target, they had to be brought home, rather than dropped safely in the sea. This presented an additional risk to both plane and crew.

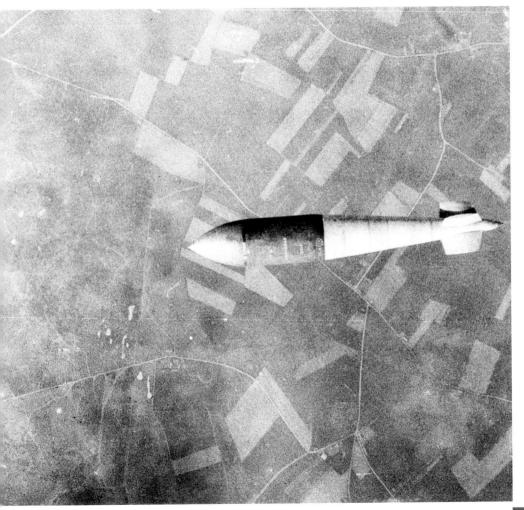

Below: *The attack on the German battleship* Tirpitz, *moored in Kaa Fjord, Norway, by Avro Lancasters of 9 and 617 Squadrons flying from bases in northern Russia. Here, a Lancaster flies towards the target (arrowed, upper left) as a colossal smoke screen is belatedly released by the German defenders. The* Tirpitz *was damaged by one hit and several near misses by 12,000lb deep penetration 'Tallboy' bombs and was subsequently moved to an anchorage further south in Norway.*

As they were so expensive, Tallboys were only used against high-value strategic targets that could not be destroyed by conventional means. They were first used successfully on the night of 8 June 1944, when 19 Lancasters of 617 Squadron carrying Tallboys, along with six carrying conventional bomb loads, attacked the Saumur railway tunnel in the Loire Valley. One Tallboy sliced through the hillside and exploded in the tunnel about 60 feet below, knocking out the only rail line running north–south in the Loire.

They were used in Operation Crossbow against V-1 and V-2 rocket installations, then against German dockyards, canals and U-boat pens. Most famously they were used against the German battleship *Tirpitz*, which was hidden in a Norwegian fjord. Lancasters carrying Tallboys made three attempts to sink her in the autumn of 1944. They eventually succeeded on 12 November, when at least two Tallboys hit her and she capsized.

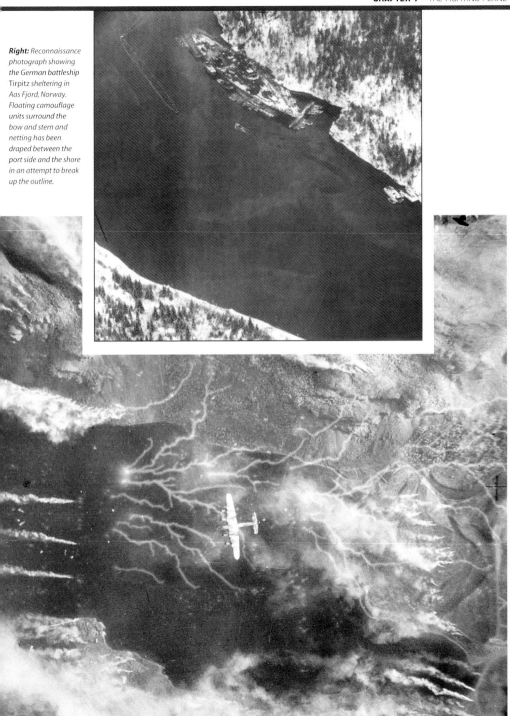

Right: Reconnaissance photograph showing the German battleship Tirpitz *sheltering in Aas Fjord, Norway. Floating camouflage units surround the bow and stern and netting has been draped between the port side and the shore in an attempt to break up the outline.*

Above: *Further daylight attacks on the* Tirpitz, *which is moored at Haakoy, near Tromso, Norway. The aerial photograph shows a large column of smoke rising from the ship (upper right) after being hit by 12,000lb deep penetration 'Tallboy' bombs. A photographic-reconnaissance sortie, 2¹/₂ hours after the attack, confirmed that the battleship had capsized at her moorings.*

Below: There was to be no hiding from British bombers. The Tirpitz is seen lying capsized in Tromso Fjord, attended by a salvage vessel. The already damaged ship was finally sunk in a combined daylight attack by 9 and 617 Squadrons on 12 November 1944. The hole in the hull by the starboard propeller shaft was cut by the Germans to allow access by salvage crews.

But Barnes Wallis was not finished. He then developed the 22,000lb Grand Slam bomb. This was closer to the huge earthquake bomb Barnes Wallis had originally envisaged. Again, it was dropped by a Lancaster. To carry the bomb, which was 25 feet 6 inches long, the Lancaster had to be substantially modified, producing the Mark I (Special). Modifications including the removal of all the cockpit armour plating, and the mid-upper turret and two guns from the rear turret. Rolls-Royce Merlin 24 engines were installed. These gave better take-off performance. The rear end of the bomb bay was cut away to clear the bomb tail and the bomb-bay doors were removed. Later the nose turret was removed to lighten the plane still further.

Grand Slam bombs were dropped on V-2 facilities, railway viaducts and U-boat pens. On 14 March 1945, the earthquake caused by a Grand Slam dropped from 16,000 feet on the railway at Bielefeld made 100 yards of viaduct collapse. At Brest, Grand Slams penetrated the 30-foot concrete ceilings of the U-boat pens.

Essentially the Grand Slam was an enlarged Tallboy; both were made by Vickers in Sheffield. Like the Tallboy, the Grand Slam's fins gave it a spin for stability and accuracy. Its casing was also thicker than a conventional bomb. Only 9,135lb of its weight was explosive. Again Torpex was used, giving a blast equivalent to 6.5 tons of TNT. The Grand Slam was handmade and even more expensive than the Tallboy, so any not used on a sortie had to be brought home. However, while 854 Tallboys were used, only 41 Grand Slams were dropped during the war.

Left: Twenty aircraft took part in the raid on the bridge at Nienburg, Germany, and the target was destroyed. The bomb in the photograph is displayed at the Battle of Britain Memorial Fund visitor centre at Coningsby, Lincolnshire.

Above: A 22,000lb MC high explosive, deep-penetration bomb (Bomber Command executive codeword 'Grand Slam') is manoeuvred onto a trolley by crane in the bomb dump at Woodhall Spa, Lincolnshire, for an evening raid by 617 Squadron on the railway bridge at Nienburg, Germany.

Below: *Lancaster I (Special) PD119/YZ-J, of 617 Squadron. One of 33 aircraft modified in February 1945 to carry the 22,000lb 'Grand Slam', deep-penetration bomb.*

Right: *Avro Lancaster B Mark I (Special), PB996 YZ-C, of 617 Squadron RAF, flown by Flying Officer P Martin and crew, releasing a 22,000lb MC deep-penetration bomb, 'Grand Slam', over the viaduct at Arnsberg, Germany.*

Below: *A photo-reconnaissance view of the twin railway viaducts at Schildesche, Bielefeld, Germany, following the successful daylight attack by 15 Avro Lancasters of 617 Squadron, on 14 March 1945. Five arches of the viaducts collapsed after 22,000lb 'Grand Slam' and 12,000lb 'Tallboy' deep penetration bombs were dropped in the target area. Numerous craters from previous attempts to demolish the structure can be seen covering the floor of the Johannisbach Valley.*

In all Lancasters carried out a total of 156,000 missions during the war, dropping 608,612 tons of high-explosive bombs and more than 51 million incendiaries. Because the Lancaster could carry a larger bomb load, it dropped around double the tonnage of bombs delivered by the Handley Page Halifax, the other major bomber used by the RAF. However, there was a price to pay. In its four years of combat service, 3,249 Lancasters were lost in action and another 487 were destroyed or damaged while on the ground. Only 24 Lancasters completed more than a hundred missions.

Below: Wellington IC, R1448/HA-L, of 218 (Gold Coast) Squadron, in August 1941.

Gun Turrets

The FN5 was a gun turret designed to replace the original Barnes Wallis turrets used at the front and rear of the Wellington Mark I bomber in the run-up to World War II. The same turret was later used as the nose turret of the Manchester, Stirling and Lancaster bombers. In all, over 22,000 FN5 turrets were produced – more than any other turret in the war.

The FN5 carried two 0.303-inch Browning Mark II machine guns, with 1,000 rounds a gun when used as a front turret and 2,000 rounds a gun as a rear turret where no provision had to be made for the bomb aimer. The guns were located to either side of the gunner, giving easy access in case of blockage or other problems.

On the Wellington, the front turret suffered from some vibration and affected the flight characteristics of the aircraft when it was fully turned to the side. Even so, the FN5 was used for both front and rear turrets on the Wellington IA, IC and II. It was replaced by the four-gun FN20 rear turret on the Wellington III.

Left: A Vickers Wellington Mark IC of 38 Squadron, at Shallufa, Egypt, receives a check-out and clean-up.

Below: *Veteran air gunner Flt Lt J A Howard DFC
in the rear turret of a 619 Squadron Lancaster.*

The Manchester, Stirling and Lancaster used the FN5 as a front turret, while the four-gun version was fitted at the rear, where the danger of attack was higher. Later models had the FN120 turret, fitted with the Village Inn gun-laying radar. A few had Rose Rice turrets with two .50-calibre Brownings.

There was not enough space in the turret for the gunner to wear his parachute and operate the turret properly, so the gunner's parachute was left in the fuselage just outside the turret. If he needed to abandon ship, he had to turn the turret fully forward, then open the door and grab his parachute. After closing the door, he had to rotate the turret fully to one side. Then he opened the door and fell backwards out of the turret. This was nerve-racking enough for the rear gunner, but the front gunner risked falling into the propellers.

While the turret was moved hydraulically by the gunner, it could also be rotated manually from inside the aircraft. This allowed other crew members to rescue a trapped or wounded gunner.

Below: *As can be seen here, there is little room for the rear gunner to move around. The guns can be seen either side along with their controls.*

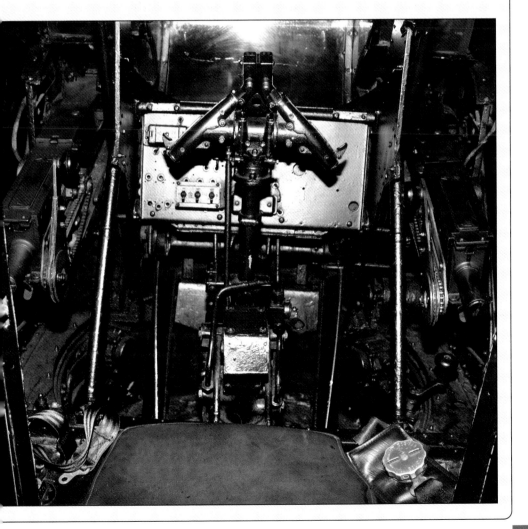

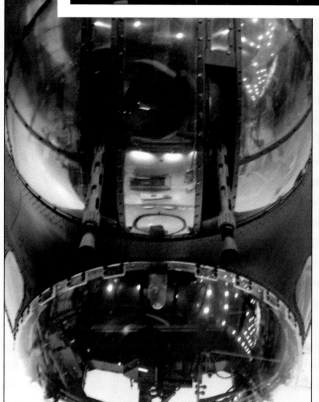

Above: *These are the guns inside the front gunner position. The bomb aimer played two roles, firstly as the bomb aimer, but also when he wasn't doing that he would act as the front gunner. Squeezing himself into the upper part of the front section, right above where his bombing position was, he would then have access to this tiny front gunners' area. Shown here (left) is the gunner's position at the top and the bomb aimer's position at the bottom.*

The Browning Machine Gun

The Browning 0.303-inch Mark II machine gun was the standard weapon used in the gun turrets on most British bombers during World War II. The gun was selected after competitive tests in 1934. It was essentially the American 1930 Pattern belt-fed Colt-Browning machine gun with a few minor modifications for use with British ammunition. Both Vickers and BSA were given a licence to produce the gun, and by the outbreak of war production was running flat out.

In combat, it was found that the muzzle extension was prone to fouling. This was because far more rounds were loosed off than in testing. Cooling fins were added to the muzzle extension and it was chrome-plated to make the surface smoother. This modified version, the Mark II, remained the standard gun used in British bombers for most of the war.

While the Americans fitted .50-inch machine guns to their bombers and fighter aircraft were increasingly using 20mm cannon, the British stuck with the .303. This was because, while the longer range of the heavier guns may have been useful in the daylight operations that the Americans undertook, it was of little benefit on British night-time raids, at least until gun-laying radar was introduced.

The Browning Mark II was also accurate, reliable and available in large numbers. Another advantage was that the lighter gun used lighter ammunition. A .303 bullet weighed 0.4 ounces, while the .50 weighed more than three times as much at 1.4 ounces. That meant, with the bigger gun, you could either carry less ammunition or cut the bomb load. It was only towards the end of 1944, when they expected to undertake daylight operations, that the RAF begin to fit 0.50 calibre machine guns to their Lancasters.

Browning .303 Statistics

Calibre: 0.303 inches

Weight: 21lb 14oz

Length: 3 feet 8.5 inches

Maximum range: 3,000 feet

Rate of fire: 1,150 rounds a minute

Muzzle velocity: 2,660 feet per second

Right: *Depicted here are the two Browning guns from a four-gun turret. This is just one side of the turret, which would have the same configuration on the other side.*

Above: Photo-reconnaissance view of part of Cologne before the area-bombing attacks by aircraft of Bomber Command, showing a 230-acre area of the southern Altstadt. The Neumarkt is seen at centre left and the Mauritius-Kirche at lower centre.

Area Bombing

On 22 September 1941, the RAF issued a memo recommending area bombing. Known as the 'Dehousing Paper', it read:

"Careful analysis of the effects of raids on Birmingham, Hull and elsewhere have shown that, on the average, 1 ton of bombs dropped on a built-up area demolishes 20–40 dwellings and turns 100–200 people out of house and home. We know from our experience that we can count on nearly 14 operational sorties per bomber produced. The average lift of the bombers we are going to produce over the next 15 months will be about 3 tons. It follows that each of these bombers will in its life-time drop about 40 tons of bombs. If these are dropped on built-up areas they will make 4,000–8,000 people homeless. In 1938 over 22 million Germans lived in 58 towns of over 100,000 inhabitants, which, with modern equipment, should be easy to find and hit. Our forecast output of heavy bombers (including Wellingtons) between now and the middle of 1943 is about 10,000. If even half the total load of 10,000 bombers were dropped on the built-up areas of these 58 German towns the great majority of their inhabitants (about one-third of the German population) would be turned out of house and home. Investigation seems to show that having one's home demolished is most damaging to morale. People seem to mind it more than having their friends or even relatives killed. At Hull signs of strain were evident, though only one-tenth of the houses were demolished. On the above figures we should be able to do ten times as much harm to each of the 58 principal German towns. There seems little doubt that this would break the spirit of the people."

A month after this memo was written, the first production model of the Lancaster took to the air. This great bomber was used to carry out the strategy.

Thousand-Bomber Raid

When Air Marshal Arthur 'Bomber' Harris took over in February 1942, he felt that Bomber Command had yet to prove its worth, so he planned a bombing raid on a German city that would be so devastating, he believed the German people would force their leaders to sue for peace. For propaganda purposes, he wanted the raid to be carried out by 1,000 planes. By then there were six squadrons of Lancaster bombers ready to take part in the raid.

It was a daring plan and new tactics had to be devised to minimize the possibility of mid-air collisions. Harris wanted to bomb Hamburg, a vital sea port. Churchill favoured Essen, the centre of German industry. But the strategists advised that Cologne would be a better target as it was closer to home and, as a rail hub, its destruction would make it difficult for Germany to move men and equipment around.

At 2230 on May 30, a thousand bombers began taking off from 53 bases across Britain. Once over the Continent, crews were told to look for the Rhine and follow it until they reached Cologne. The planes flew above the clouds over Western Europe, but these cleared over the city, which was bathed in the light of a full moon.

More than 2,000 tons of bombs were dropped – four times the amount dropped on the worst night of the Blitz. Within 15 minutes, the old town was ablaze. The glow of the flames could be seen a hundred miles away and smoke rose 15,000 feet in the air. It was so dense that the RAF could not get any usable reconnaissance photos of the city for a week. Six hundred acres of the city had been razed, 13,000 homes destroyed, another 6,000 badly damaged, and 45,000 people made homeless. Some 469 were killed and over 5,000 badly wounded. Of the 1,046 bombers that took part in the raid, 39 were lost – four in mid-air collisions over the target, the rest mainly to night fighters. It was a loss of 4 per cent, which was considered the maximum Bomber Command could sustain. However, although Cologne was paralyzed for a week, within six months it had recovered and Germany did not surrender. Indeed, within hours the Luftwaffe had mounted a bombing raid of their own on the historic city of Canterbury.

Above: *Photo-reconnaissance view taken over Cologne, Germany, after 'Operation Millennium', the first 'Thousand-bomber' raid by aircraft of Bomber Command on the night of 30/31 May 1942. This view shows widespread damage on either side of Luxemburger Strasse.*

Under the Bombs

On 21 June 1945, a 21-year-old woman who worked in the Focke-Wulf munitions factory in Bremen was interviewed by the occupying forces about the effects of carpet bombing on German morale. She told her interrogators:

"In the early part of the war, alarms came well ahead of attacks; one had an hour or more to get to the shelter. But later on the alarms came at the same time as the fliers themselves or only a couple of minutes sooner. The air-raid shelters were too few and too small. The one which we used where I live was intended for 800 people and was actually used by three or four thousand. In there we were so crowded and hot that one after another vomited and the air became worse on that account. We just took off our clothes without shame because of the unbearable heat…"

During a massive raid on 6 October 1944 she managed to persuade the official at the door of the bunker to let her go out to see whether she could save her home.

"Outside all was a sea of flames. The house next to ours was in flames. You couldn't see that there were any flames in our house because of the air-raid curtains. It was difficult to get to my house because of the air raid and across the way a house had had a direct hit and was blocking the entrance somewhat. I got inside and ran upstairs. As I got in, a wave of smoke met me. Several incendiary bombs had penetrated the attic. I threw sand on them and extinguished them. Also a bed had caught on fire. I threw it out of the window. I had to go downstairs then because it was difficult to breathe up there. Downstairs I got a wet cloth to hold on my nose; luckily the water was running. I ran back to the shelter to get my mother because I could not handle the whole situation alone. Again I had difficulty with the official at the gate. He said: 'Either in or out.' Nevertheless, I succeeded in causing him to make another exception in my favour. Then I went back home with my mother, for whom I had also brought additional wet cloths. When we got home a new wave of bombers passed overhead, but we went ahead with our fire-fighting. My mother found and extinguished some incendiary bombs, or rather we both extinguished them. The windows were blown open by pressure from the demolition bombs which had struck earlier, and showers of sparks from the surrounding flames had set fire to the curtains and rug. I tore down the curtains and threw them out of the window. My mother ran and fetched water from the bathtub which we always kept handy and with that she put out the fire in the rug. After we had things under control, my mother went back to the bunker and I stayed home as long as I could stand it, but the air was so hot from all the flames everywhere that I got dizzy and got a headache, so I went back to the bunker… I went back and forth between the bunker and my home all night long. In our street one house after another burned. The fire-fighters were not to be seen. Fire engines were there from all cities around Bremen. They stood around idly for a long time, saying they could not couple the hose to the hydrant without an order to that effect. In time, however, they got such an order no doubt, because they helped put out the fire in the house on the other side of mine. I, too, helped, of course, and also kept pouring water on the walls of my house, which were very hot, so as to keep the flames from spreading. I worked in this way all night at one thing or another. In the morning I worked to mop up the water damage to our house, when I was interrupted at 10 o'clock by an alarm."

Right: *An aerial view of part of the devastated Walle district of Bremen, looking southeast towards the Altstadt. Note the large, undamaged, public air-raid shelter (Luftschutzbunker), standing on Zwinglistrasse in the foreground. Between the nights of 17/18 May 1940 and 22/23 April 1945, Bomber Command dropped over 12,800 tons of bombs on the city, causing firestorms that killed thousands.*

Left: A Sherman tank and infantry advance into a heavily bombed area of Bremen, 26 April 1945.

Chapter Eight

Operational History

The Avro Lancaster spent almost the whole of its wartime career with Bomber Command, and Sir Arthur 'Bomber' Harris fought any attempt to divert his four-engined heavy bombers from the job of carpet-bombing German cities. When he was forced to hand over planes to other branches of the RAF, such as Coastal Command, he would send Halifaxes or Stirlings. Consequently, the Lancaster became the plane most associated with the bombing campaign against Germany. It dropped close to two-thirds of Bomber Command's total tonnage of bombs during the entire war.

After their first mission, laying mines off Heligoland, the Lancasters of 44 Squadron joined the first raid on Essen. Then on 20 March, the Lancasters of 97 Squadron went into action over Germany. However, the existence of the Lancaster was kept secret until a low-level raid on Augsburg on 17 April 1942. The target was the Maschinenfabrik Augsburg Nürnburg, a factory that made diesel engines for U-boats. This meant the Lancasters would have to cross some 1,000 miles of enemy-held territory in broad daylight.

Left: *Lancaster B Mark I, L7578 KM-B of 97 Squadron. This is being piloted a by Squadron Leader J D Nettleton of 44 Squadron, flying low over the Lincolnshire countryside during a Squadron practice for the low-level attack on the MAN diesel engineering works at Augsburg, Germany, which took place on 17 April 1942. 97 Squadron loaned L7578 to 44 Squadron on a temporary basis and they repainted the aircraft with Nettleton's unit code-letters. Nettleton actually flew R5508 on the operation, for the leadership of which he was awarded the Victoria Cross. L7578 did not participate in the raid and was returned to 97 Squadron at Woodhall Spa.*

Left: *The Acting Commanding Officer of 44 Squadron, Squadron Leader J D Nettleton (seated, second from left) and his crew, photographed on their return to Waddington, Lincolnshire, England, after leading the low-level daylight attack on the MAN diesel engineering works at Augsburg on 17 April 1942. For his courage and leadership during the raid Nettleton was gazetted for the award of the Victoria Cross on 28 April. He later commanded 44 Squadron, but was killed on 13 July 1943 while returning from a raid on Turin, Italy.*

The raid was to be led by Squadron Leader John Nettleton from RAF Waddington. On the morning of 17 April ground crews fuelled and armed eight Lancasters of 44 Squadron, though one was kept on standby. Their tanks were filled with their maximum capacity of 2,154 gallons and four 1,000lb general purpose high-explosive bombs, fitted with 11-second delay detonators, were hoisted into each aircraft bomb bay. Take-off for the raid was set for mid-afternoon.

At 1512 hours the Lancasters lifted off. Once they were all airborne, the last Lancaster circled and returned to base. It had been a second standby. The remaining six Lancasters formed up in two three-plane 'Vs' and headed south across Lincolnshire. Over Selsey Bill, they were joined by six more Lancasters from 97 Squadron, based at Woodhall Spa, under the command of Squadron Leader J S Sherwood DFC. All 12 dropped to 50 feet as they roared across the English Channel. Ahead of them, 30 USAAF Boston bombers and some 800 fighters were bombing and strafing targets away from the bombers' route in the hope of drawing off the Luftwaffe.

By the time they reached the French coast, Nettleton's section had drawn ahead of Sherwood's. As it was vital to preserve fuel on such a long trip, Sherwood did not try to catch up. The briefing had made it clear that they could make two separate attacks if necessary.

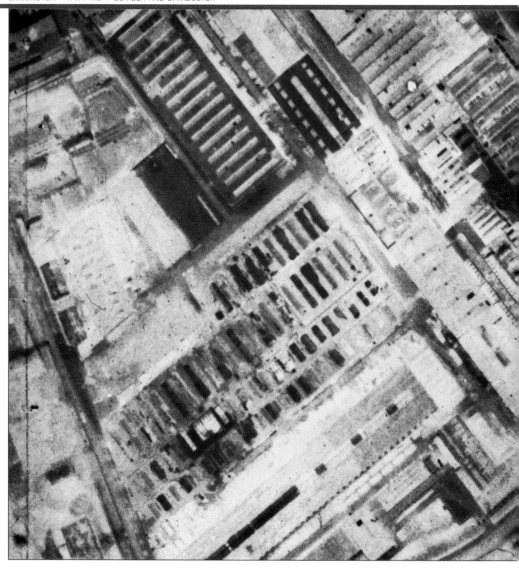

As they crossed the coast into enemy-occupied territory, they met no serious opposition from ground defences and none from the Luftwaffe. But then Nettleton got into trouble. Now well ahead of the 97 Squadron formation, they were skirting the airfield at Beaumont le Roger when they spotted a number of German aircraft coming in to land after dogfights off Cherbourg. For a moment Nettleton's men thought they had not been spotted, but then the German fighters snapped up their undercarriages, aborting their landing, and turned towards them.

First they attacked the rear V formation. A hail of cannon shells hit L7565 V flown by Warrant Officer J E Beckett. His Lancaster burst into flames and crashed into a clump of trees. All four engines of Flight Lieutenant N Sandford's R5506 P were on fire when the plane exploded. The port wing of Warrant Officer H V Crum's plane, L7548 T, erupted in flames. He jettisoned his bomb load immediately and put the crippled Lancaster down, as he had been told during the briefing, saving some of the crew. The fighters now moved on to the front three Lancasters.

Left: *Enlargement of an aerial reconnaissance photograph, showing damage to the main diesel-engine assembly workshop in the MAN factory at Augsburg, Germany, following the notable low-level attack by Avro Lancasters of No 5 Group, Bomber Command on 17 April 1942.*

Major Oesau, a hundred-victory ace forbidden to fly more operations, had jumped into a fighter and taken off on first sight of the Lancasters. He closed to within 10 yards of Warrant Officer G T Rhodes' Lancaster, L7536 H, guns blazing. The bomber's port engines both erupted in flames, followed by the starboard engines. The Lancaster reared, stalled and plunged straight down, narrowly missing the other two planes. However, it was then the fighters ran out of fuel, so Nettleton in R5508 B and Flying Officer J Garwell DFC DFM in R5505 P continued their journey, although both planes were damaged. Nevertheless they reached the target. They ran in, in close formation, and released their bombs. But on the run-out, Garwell's plane was hit by anti-aircraft fire. With the plane belching smoke and flames, Garwell put the Lancaster down, saving the lives of all but three of his crew. Nettleton, whose plane was full of holes, turned for home alone in the hope that the gathering dusk might offer some form of protection.

Sherwood's six Lancasters were now approaching the target, which was now well marked by the smoke from the initial attack. They formed a line astern and went in at rooftop level. After dropping their bombs, they dropped to street level in an attempt to get under the flak curtain. It was an impossible task. Sherwood's Lancaster was hit and burst into flames. It flew straight into the ground and exploded.

Two of the Lancasters in the second formation were hit on the run-in. Although his plane was a ball of fire Warrant Officer Mycock DFC in Lancaster R5513 P continued the attack, but then the plane exploded in mid-air. The other burning bomber, skippered by Flying Officer E A Deverill, completed its bombing run and pulled away, even though it was trailing flames from one engine. The fire was extinguished, but the plane also bore a 10-foot gash along the fuselage. Nevertheless, it managed to form up with the other survivors from 97 Squadron and headed back to base. Of the 12 aircraft that had set out on the mission, only 5 returned and 49 of the 85 men were missing. John Nettleton was awarded the Victoria Cross, the first Lancaster crewman to receive it. He was shot down over the Bay of Biscay on 13 July 1943. His body was never recovered.

Above: *Vertical aerial reconnaissance photograph taken over Cologne, Germany before the first thousand-bomber raid of 30/31 May 1942. The photograph shows the city area south of the cathedral (bottom left).*

Although the Lancaster was soon proving its worth, it did not outnumber the other aircraft in Bomber Command until February 1943. In early 1942, when 'Bomber' Harris was planning the first thousand-bomber raid, the most common aircraft was still the twin-engined Vickers Wellington medium bomber. In the raid against Cologne on 30 May 1942, there were only 75 Lancasters compared with over 600 Wellingtons. However, the Lancaster could carry a much greater bomb load and gradually took over as the Wellington was phased out.

In August 1942, the Pathfinder Force was formed. The idea of the Pathfinders was that their experienced crews would find the target and mark it with flares. This would give the rest of the bomber force coming in behind a better chance of dropping their bombs in the right place. To start with, one Pathfinder squadron of each type of bomber was used – with 83 Squadron representing the Lancaster.

By early 1943, the Pathfinders had begun to show their worth and Bomber Command began its all-out area bombing of Germany. To help, the Pathfinders began to operate a series of navigation aids, starting with Oboe. Among its many drawbacks, it could not work as far away as Berlin or Hamburg due to the curvature of the earth. The planes equipped with Oboe had to fly straight and level for extended periods, making them vulnerable to attack.

Left: Part of the locomotive shop of the Krupps AG works at Essen, Germany, seriously damaged by Bomber Command in 1943, and further wrecked in the daylight raid of 11 March 1945.

On 5 March 1943, Oboe was used in the attack on the Krupps works at Essen. Essen and the Ruhr would suffer six major attacks between then and 25 July. Duisburg would also suffer a series of major raids. By that time, 18 squadrons of Bomber Command were equipped with Lancasters and it had taken over as the Command's most numerous bomber.

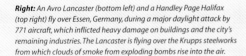

Right: An Avro Lancaster (bottom left) and a Handley Page Halifax (top right) fly over Essen, Germany, during a major daylight attack by 771 aircraft, which inflicted heavy damage on buildings and the city's remaining industries. The Lancaster is flying over the Krupps steelworks from which clouds of smoke from exploding bombs rise into the air.

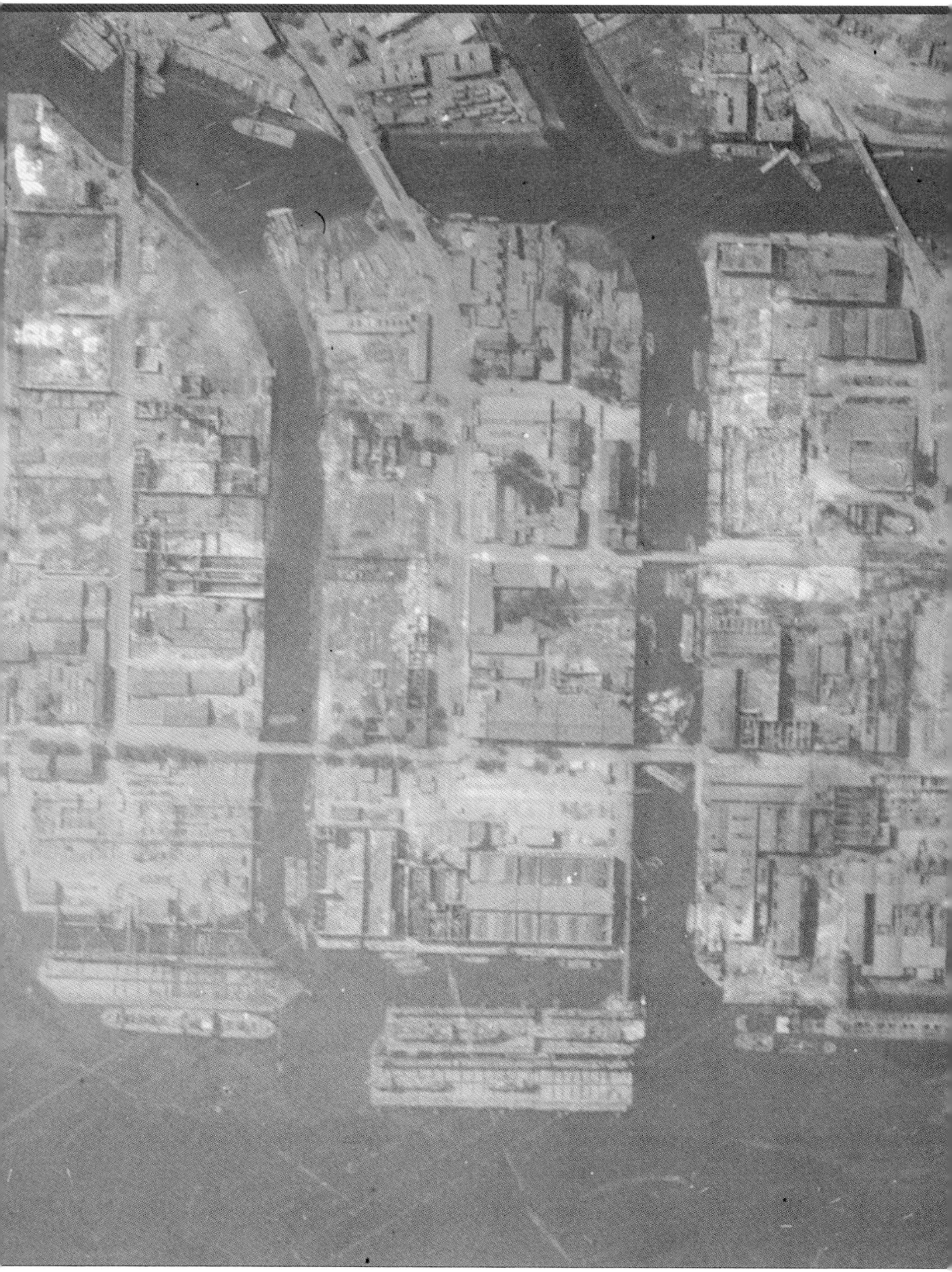

Then in May came the Dambusters raid. Although knocking out the Ruhr dams did not have the economic impact the RAF had hoped for, it demonstrated the capabilities of Allied air power and was a huge propaganda victory.

The next target was Hamburg. It was a particularly tempting target for Bomber Command. The battleship *Bismarck*, then safely at the bottom of the Atlantic, had been built there, along with some 200 U-boats. The new H2S system of downward-facing radar was used to pick out the built-up areas. On this raid, Bomber Command also deployed 'Windows' for the first time. Strips of aluminium foil were dropped to disrupt German radar.

For the first time, the US Eighth Air Force were invited to join a Bomber Command campaign. B-17 Fortresses would fly 252 daylight sorties in the two days following the first of four RAF night raids. While Bomber Command concentrated on area bombing, the Americans would pick out key industrial targets.

Four major raids would take place in the space of ten nights in what was known as Operation Gomorrah. They began on 24 July when the outskirts of Hamburg were bombed. Out of the 740 RAF bombers sent, only 12 were lost. The following day, 68 American B-17s struck Hamburg's U-boat pens and shipyards. The day after that, another American attack destroyed the city's power plant.

The high point of the operation came on the night of 27 July when 787 aircraft – 353 Lancasters, 244 Halifaxes, 116 Stirlings and 74 Wellingtons – made it back to base. The American commander, Brigadier-General Anderson, flew in a Lancaster to watch the raid. The centre of the Pathfinder marking was about two miles east of the centre of the city. The 787 aircraft dropped 2,326 tons of bombs in a tightly packed area. It is estimated that 550 to 600 bomb loads fell into an area measuring just 2 square miles.

Left: A mosaic of aerial reconnaissance photographs taken of Hamburg, Germany, after major raids by aircraft of Bomber Command on the nights of 27/28 July and 29/30 July 1943. Severe damage can be seen to buildings from the St Georg district through the Hammerbrook, Borgfeld and Hamm districts.

It was a warm evening and it had not rained for some time, so everything was very dry. The concentrated bombing caused a large number of fires in the densely built-up working-class districts of Hammerbrook, Hamm and Borgfeld. Most of Hamburg's fire vehicles had been in the western parts of the city, damping down the fires still smouldering there from the raid three nights earlier and the roads were blocked by the rubble caused by high-explosive 'cookies' the Lancasters had dropped early in the raid.

About half-way through the attack, the fires in Hammerbrook started joining together, sucking in the surrounding air. The resulting firestorm caused 150mph winds and temperatures of 1,800 degrees. Even the asphalt caught fire and onlookers were swept into the flames. The bombing continued for another half hour, spreading the firestorm area gradually eastwards. The firestorm raged for about 3 hours and only subsided when all combustible material had been consumed.

The burnt-out area was almost entirely residential. Around 16,000 apartment buildings had been destroyed, razing around 10 square miles. There were few survivors from the firestorm area and approximately 40,000 people were dead. Most of them had suffocated when the oxygen was sucked out of the basements where they were sheltering. Over a million people had been made homeless.

On the Allied side, the raid was considered a success. The RAF had dropped over 8,000 tons of bombs and lost only 17 aircraft – 11 Lancasters, 4 Halifaxes, 1 Stirling, 1 Wellington – just 2.2 per cent of the force.

Immediately following the raid, some 1,200,000 people – two-thirds of the population of Hamburg – fled the city in fear of further raids. Indeed, the RAF continued their night raids for another week, though the Americans had stopped after the first two nights. Smoke from the fires started by the RAF raids made it impossible to find their targets.

The next major target was Berlin. The city was well defended and raids in the German capital would be costly. "It will cost us between 400 and 500 aircraft," said 'Bomber' Harris. "It will cost Germany the war."

By the autumn of 1943, he could deploy over 800 long-range bombers on any given night, equipped with new and more sophisticated navigational devices such as H2S radar. After high losses among Halifaxes and Stirlings in late August and early September, the Lancaster would take the lead. Between November 1943 and March 1944 they made 16 massed attacks on Berlin.

Right: An aerial photograph taken during the night raid on Hamburg of 24/25 July 1943. Sticks of incendiaries can be seen burning in the Altona and Dock districts (top). A photoflash bomb at lower left has illuminated the camouflaged Binnen Alster and the Aussen Alster on which a flak position had been built.

Left: A Lancaster crew of 467 Squadron, Royal Australian Air Force (RAAF), at Bottesford, Leicestershire, England, preparing to set off for Berlin, Germany, on the evening of 31 August 1943. From the left: Flight Sergeants J Scott, G Eriksen and A Boys, Sergeant C Adair, Flight Sergeant B Jones (Captain), Flight Sergeant J Wilkinson and Sergeant E Tull, RAF, the only Englishman in the crew.

On the night of 18 November, Berlin was attacked by 440 Lancasters, led by 4 de Havilland Mosquitoes. The city was under cloud and the damage was not severe. However, a second major raid on the night of 22 November was the RAF's most effective raid on Berlin of the war. A total of 764 aircraft – 469 Lancasters, 234 Halifaxes, 50 Stirlings and 11 Mosquitoes – went in for the kill. Again it had been dry, and firestorms were started, causing extensive damage to the residential areas west of the centre of the city. Some 2,000 Berliners were killed, and another 175,000 made homeless. A number of key buildings were destroyed, including the Ministry of Munitions and several arms factories. Some 26 aircraft were lost, 3.4 per cent of the attack force.

The following night, Berlin was attacked by 365 Lancasters, 10 Halifaxes and 8 Mosquitoes. Another 1,000 Berliners were killed and 100,000 made homeless. There were small raids for the next two nights, then on the night of 26 November, 443 Lancasters and 7 Mosquitoes returned. Most of the damage in Berlin was in the semi-industrial suburb of Reinickendorf. Stuttgart was also attacked by 84 aircraft that night. The total sorties for the night was 666; 34 aircraft (5.1 per cent) were lost.

Left: The Siemens factory at Siemensstadt, Berlin, Germany, badly damaged as a result of raids by aircraft of Bomber Command.

Small attacks continued nightly until 2 December when 425 Lancasters, 15 Halifaxes and 18 Mosquitoes returned to Berlin. But German fighters were waiting. Cross-winds scattered the bomber formations and the Luftwaffe downed 40 bombers – 37 Lancasters, 2 Halifaxes and 1 Mosquito, a massive 8.7 per cent of the force. The cross-winds also made the bombing inaccurate. However, two Siemens factories, a ball-bearing factory and several railway installations were damaged.

Another 483 Lancasters and 15 Mosquitoes were sent to Berlin on the night of 16 December. Again German night fighters successfully intercepted the bombers. Some 25 Lancasters – 5.2 per cent of the Lancaster force – were lost over enemy-occupied territory. A further 29 aircraft were lost on landing in England due to very low cloud. However, more damage was done to the railway system in Berlin and a thousand wagon-loads of war material destined for the Eastern Front were delayed for six days. A number of important buildings, including the National Theatre and Germany's military and political archives, were destroyed. By that time more than a quarter of Berlin's living accommodation was uninhabitable.

Below: *Heavily laden Avro Lancaster B Mark IIIs of 106 Squadron taxi from their dispersals to the head of runway 20 at Metheringham, Lincolnshire, for take-off on a raid to Frankfurt, Germany. The resulting attack on 22/23 March 1944 caused extensive destruction to eastern, central and western districts of the city, including the Opera House and the preserved medieval quarter.*

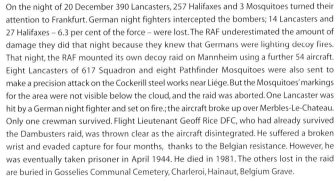

Left: Armourers prepare to load 1,000lb MC bombs into the bomb bay of an Avro Lancaster B Mark III of 106 Squadron at Metheringham, Lincolnshire, for a major night raid on Frankfurt, Germany. The chalk markings on the bombs indicate that each has been fused with a Number 43 air-armed nose pistol, the safety pins of which can be seen hanging from the nose rotor. These would be removed shortly before the crew board the aircraft.

On the night of 20 December 390 Lancasters, 257 Halifaxes and 3 Mosquitoes turned their attention to Frankfurt. German night fighters intercepted the bombers; 14 Lancasters and 27 Halifaxes – 6.3 per cent of the force – were lost. The RAF underestimated the amount of damage they did that night because they knew that Germans were lighting decoy fires. That night, the RAF mounted its own decoy raid on Mannheim using a further 54 aircraft. Eight Lancasters of 617 Squadron and eight Pathfinder Mosquitoes were also sent to make a precision attack on the Cockerill steel works near Liége. But the Mosquitoes' markings for the area were not visible below the cloud, and the raid was aborted. One Lancaster was hit by a German night fighter and set on fire.; the aircraft broke up over Merbles-Le-Chateau. Only one crewman survived. Flight Lieutenant Geoff Rice DFC, who had already survived the Dambusters raid, was thrown clear as the aircraft disintegrated. He suffered a broken wrist and evaded capture for four months, thanks to the Belgian resistance. However, he was eventually taken prisoner in April 1944. He died in 1981. The others lost in the raid are buried in Gosselies Communal Cemetery, Charleroi, Hainaut, Belgium Grave.

There were raids on two flying-bomb sites at Amiens and Abbeville on 22 December. One was destroyed; the other not located. The following night 364 Lancasters, 7 Halifaxes and 8 Mosquitoes returned to Berlin. The weather gave German fighters some difficulties but they were able to shoot down only 16 Lancasters, 4.2 per cent of the force. The weather hampered the Lancasters also, and the damage they inflicted on Berlin was relatively light.

The relentless assault on Berlin continued on the night of 28 December when 457 Lancasters, 252 Halifaxes and 3 Mosquitoes arrived above the city. Heavy cloud cover frustrated the bombers and damage was slight. Twenty planes were lost, but at only 2.8 per cent of the force, this was considered light.

On the night of 30 December ten Lancasters of 617 Squadron led by six Pathfinder Mosquitoes attacked a V-1 site, but failed to destroy it. On 1 January 421 Lancasters were over Berlin again, but German night fighters shot down 28, a massive 6.7 per cent of the bombers. Nevertheless, the following night 362 Lancasters, 9 Halifaxes and 12 Mosquitoes were over Berlin, where night fighters managed to down 27 of the Lancasters.

Below: Avro Lancaster B Mark I, R5729 KM-A, of 44 Squadron, runs up its engines in a dispersal at Dunholme Lodge, Lincolnshire, before setting out on a night raid to Berlin. This veteran aircraft had taken part in more than 70 operations with the Squadron since joining it in 1942. It was finally shot down with the loss of its entire crew during a raid on Braunschweig, Germany, on the night of 14/15 January 1944.

Two flying-bomb sites were attacked on the night of 4 January and the following night Stettin was also attacked. Diversionary attacks on Berlin and four other targets afforded the 348 Lancasters and 10 Halifaxes some measure of protection, and only 16 aircraft were lost, 4.5 per cent of the force.

Small attacks continued until the night of 14 January when the first major raid was launched against Brunswick by 496 Lancasters and 2 Halifaxes. Night fighters managed to down 38 Lancasters; eleven of them were Pathfinders, so the targeting of the city was poor. German authorities reported that only 14 people were killed and 10 houses destroyed in Brunswick itself, with some further loss of life and property in villages to the south of the town. Another 82 planes attacked flying-bomb sites at Ailly, Bonneton and Bristillerie without loss while 17 Mosquitoes launched small raids on Magdeburg and Berlin.

Berlin was the main target again on the night of 20 January, when 495 Lancasters, 264 Halifaxes and 10 Mosquitoes attacked. Night fighters downed 13 Lancasters and 22 Halifaxes. The following night the first major raid was made on Magdeburg.

The attack on Berlin was stepped up on the night of 27 January when 515 Lancasters and 15 Mosquitoes were sent. There was extensive damage, but decoy raids were only partially successful in diverting German night fighters as 33 Lancasters were lost, 6.4 per cent of the bombers. A further 167 sorties were flown against other targets, with one aircraft lost.

Despite the losses over the German capital, the following night, 432 Lancasters, 241 Halifaxes and 4 Mosquitoes were despatched to Berlin. There was a concentrated attack on southern and western districts. But it was covered with partial cloud and German records say that 77 places outside the city were hit. Though the main force came in over northern Denmark and there were several decoy raids, the German air defences managed to shoot down 46 aircraft, 6.8 per cent of the force.

Right: Flying Officer A E Manning and his crew gather by their aircraft, Avro Lancaster B Mark I, W4964 WS-J, of 9 Squadron, shortly after their return to Bardney, Lincolnshire, in the early hours of 6 January 1944, after a raid on Stettin in Germany.

Below: Three Lancaster B Mark IIIs of 619 Squadron, airborne from Coningsby, Lincolnshire. The aircraft in the foreground, LM418 PG-S, was destroyed in a crash-landing at Woodbridge Emergency Landing Ground after returning from the ill-fated Nuremberg raid of 30/31 March 1944 on two engines. Its crew survived the crash, but were all killed in action later.

Two nights later, 440 Lancasters, 82 Halifaxes and 12 Mosquitoes were sent to Berlin. Of these 33 were lost, 6.2 per cent of the total. A further 76 sorties were flown against other targets, with no aircraft lost. Despite the mounting aircraft losses, it was estimated that the raids made during December and January killed hundreds of people and rendered between 20,000 and 80,000 homeless each night. Still the bombing continued.

On the night of 15 February 1944, the RAF made its largest raid on Berlin, sending 561 Lancasters, 314 Halifaxes and 16 Mosquitoes to attack the city. Despite cloud cover, important war industries were hit. A diversionary raid by 24 Lancasters on Frankfurt-on-the-Oder failed to confuse the Germans and Bomber Command lost 26 Lancasters and 17 Halifaxes, 4.8 per cent of the force.

Another raid on Berlin was made on the night of 24 March, where losses amounted to 8.9 per cent after the bomber stream was scattered. Those that reached Berlin bombed well out to the south-west of the city and 72 aircraft were downed.

On 30 March the attack was diverted to Nuremberg. The first fighters appeared just before the main force of 572 Lancasters, 214 Halifaxes and 9 Mosquitoes reached the Belgian border. Over the next hour 82 bombers were shot down on their way to the target. Another 13 bombers were lost on the return flight and a further 71 badly damaged. The RAF lost 11.9 per cent of the force it had dispatched. This was Bomber Command's biggest loss of the war and effectively ended any further assault on Berlin.

These raids caused huge loss of life and immense devastation. In Berlin, nearly 4,000 were killed, 10,000 injured and 450,000 made homeless. Many more were evacuated to get them out of the way of the bombing.

Despite the devastation they caused, these bombing raids failed to achieve their objectives. German civilian morale did not collapse. The city's defences did not crumble. Essential services were maintained and war production, rather than being devastated, continued to rise until the end of 1944. Area bombing failed in its aim to win the war by destroying Germany's economy and crushing its people's will to fight.

Right: *A view of the Reichstag after the Allied bombing of Berlin.*

Right: Oblique aerial view of heavily damaged industrial and residential buildings in Nuremberg.

In these 16 major raids, Bomber Command lost more than 500 aircraft and 2,690 men over Berlin, and nearly 1,000 more became prisoners of war. The loss rate was 5.8 per cent, well above the 4 per cent thought to be the RAF's maximum sustainable operational loss rate. Around 7 per cent of Bomber Command's losses were incurred during the Berlin raids. In December 1943 alone, 11 Lancasters and their crews from 460 Squadron of the Royal Australian Air Force were lost in operations against Berlin. Another 14 were lost in January and February. At this rate Bomber Command would have been wiped out before Berlin.

The attack on Berlin did divert German military resources away from the land war. It also had an economic effect – killing and injuring workers, damaging factories and infrastructure, and forcing the Germans to fortify buildings and relocate facilities. Nevertheless, since the area bombing of Berlin did not force Germany's capitulation as Harris had hoped, it was a failure, if not a defeat.

Despite the heavy losses, Harris wanted to continue the strategic offensive, but he was ordered to break off. The Lancaster was to join in the preparations for D-Day. In the months before the Normandy landings, Bomber Command dropped over 42,000 tons of bombs on the French railway system. This was crucial as it prevented the Germans from using the railways to reinforce their forces in Normandy after D-Day.

Raids were also made in the South of France in preparation for landings there. The Lancasters of 617 Squadron were tasked with knocking out the Antheor railway viaduct that crossed the mouth of a river a few miles east from St Raphael on the Côte d'Azur. It was 540 feet long, 185 feet high and had nine arches, each with a 29-foot span, and it formed part of the coastal rail link between France and Italy.

The first attack came on 16 September 1943 when eight Lancasters from 617 Squadron and four from 619 Squadron left England, each carrying seven 1,000lb bombs. The raid was a notable failure. There were no reported hits and one Lancaster from 619 Squadron was lost.

They tried again on 11 November 1943. This time the attack was mounted by nine Lancasters, each carrying a 12,000lb bomb. Again the bombs missed the target and caused only minor damage. Some of the aircraft even attacked the wrong railway line in the next bay. The Lancasters came under fire from small ships out at sea during the raid. Rather than returning to England, the aircraft headed south to Blida in Algeria, then Rabat in Morocco.

On 12 February 1944, ten Lancasters again tried to attack the viaduct, but its defences had been improved. The attack again failed to sever the rail link. No aircraft were lost on this raid, but Squadron Leader Micky Martins and bomb aimer Flight Lieutenant Bob Hay were killed by gun fire from the bridge, while flight engineer Ivan Whittaker was injured. The plane had lost two engines. With no hope of making it back to England, it went on to land in Sardinia which was in American hands by then.

Left: An oblique aerial photograph of a destroyed E-boat pen in the Bassin de Mares at Le Havre, France, following heavy attacks by aircraft of Bomber Command prior to the port's occupation.

The Lancaster came into its own again when the Tallboy was in full production. Tallboys destroyed the Saumur railway tunnel on 8 June 1944, two days after D-Day. Again the attack prevented the Germans reinforcing the troops in Normandy. On 5 June, the Lancasters of 617 Squadron had also flown a 'spoof' raid, simulating an amphibious assault on the Pas de Calais.

After D-Day, it was also necessary to keep the Channel free of German U-boats and fast-attack E-boats. On 14 June 1944, 22 Lancasters of 617 Squadron and 3 Mosquito marker aircraft attacked the E-boat pens at Le Havre. One bomb penetrated the thick concrete roof. Two further waves of bombers finished off the job as part of the first large RAF daylight raid since the end of May 1943. The following day, 155 Lancasters, 130 Halifaxes and 12 Mosquitoes hit Boulogne harbour.

Over the next two months, Tallboys were used in Operation Crossbow against V-1 and V-2 installations. On 19 June, in a raid against Le Blockhaus, a heavily fortified V-2 launch site in northern France, 617 Squadron dropped a Tallboy 50 yards from the bunker, rendering it useless. Another Tallboy hit it again on 27 July, but did not penetrate the structure.

Left: Interior of one of the E-boat pens at Le Havre, France, showing the collapsed ferro-concrete roof, caused by 12,000lb deep-penetration 'Tallboy' bombs dropped by 617 Squadron in a daylight raid on 14 June 1944.

Left: Vertical, aerial reconnaissance photograph, showing the flying-bomb assembly and launch bunker under construction at Siracourt, France.

Below: An aerial reconnaissance photograph following the attack made by Nos 1 and 4 Groups, on 22 June 1944.

Above left: Enlargement of a section of an aerial reconnaissance photograph, showing the German secret weapon (V-3) site at Mimoyecques, near Marquise, France, after the daylight attack by aircraft of Bomber Command on 6 July 1944. The 18-foot (5.5m) thick concrete slab which covered three of the five 'England' gun shafts can be seen at centre, with the firing slots clearly visible. The large bomb craters, among the many which surround the area from previous Allied air raids, were caused by 12,000lb Tallboy deep-penetration bombs dropped by 617 Squadron during their daylight raid on 6 July 1944. Three near-misses and one direct hit on the corner of the slab (at its lower left) were enough to cause the collapse of one of the gun shafts and some of the underground tunnels. The Germans were unable to repair and complete the battery before it was overrun by the Allies the following month.

A large bunker had been built at Siracourt to store the V-1 flying bombs launched from the Pas de Calais. There were other V-1 and V-2 facilities in the area. On 22 June, 119 Lancasters, 102 Halifaxes and 13 Mosquitoes attacked the sites at Siracourt and Mimoyecques where the Germans had built their V-3, a supergun with rocket-propelled shells that could bombard London. But 617 Squadron, who were to attack a bunker called La Coupole at nearby Wizernes with Tallboys, failed to find their target because of cloud and returned without dropping their bombs. Nineteen Lancasters and three Mosquitoes had failed to find it two days before.

Returning on 24 June, they found the huge dome of La Coupole. It was 71 metres in diameter and 5 metres thick. Underground railways were to bring V-2 parts there. Once assembled, they would be shipped out on mobile launch pads and fired at a rate of 40 or 50 a day. One Lancaster was lost on the raid, but this time they dropped their Tallboys. Although they did not penetrate the dome, three Tallboy bombs hit the bunker. One burst under the edge of the dome and one hit the mouth of a rail tunnel. The entire hillside collapsed, knocking out the facility. Three more attacks were made until finally, on 17 July, 16 Lancasters dropped more Tallboys. One shifted the dome out of alignment. Two others collapsed the roof and blocked the entrance.

Also on 20 June, another 17 Lancasters from 617 Squadron, along with two Mosquitoes and one Mustang, bombed the Siracourt flying-bomb store. In all, 106 Lancasters, along with 202 Halifaxes and 15 Mosquitoes, attacked three flying-bomb sites in northern France that day. The weather was clear and it was thought that all three raids were effective.

On 29 June, 286 Lancasters and 19 Mosquitoes attacked two flying-bomb launch sites and one store. There was partial cloud cover over all the targets. While some bombing seems to have been accurate, some was scattered. Three Lancasters and two Mosquitoes were lost, including the aircraft of the master bomber, on the raid to the Siracourt site.

Above: Vertical aerial reconnaissance photograph showing the flying-bomb assembly and launch bunker at Siracourt, France, prior to the final attack on the site by 17 Avro Lancasters of 617 Squadron in the afternoon of 25 June 1944.

Right: Low-level oblique aerial photograph showing the area around the site heavily pockmarked by bomb craters from previous raids mounted in June by Bomber Command and the USAAF. In the subsequent raid 617 Squadron claimed three direct hits on the concrete store with 12,000lb 'Tallboy' bombs, following low-level marking of the target by Group Captain L Cheshire.

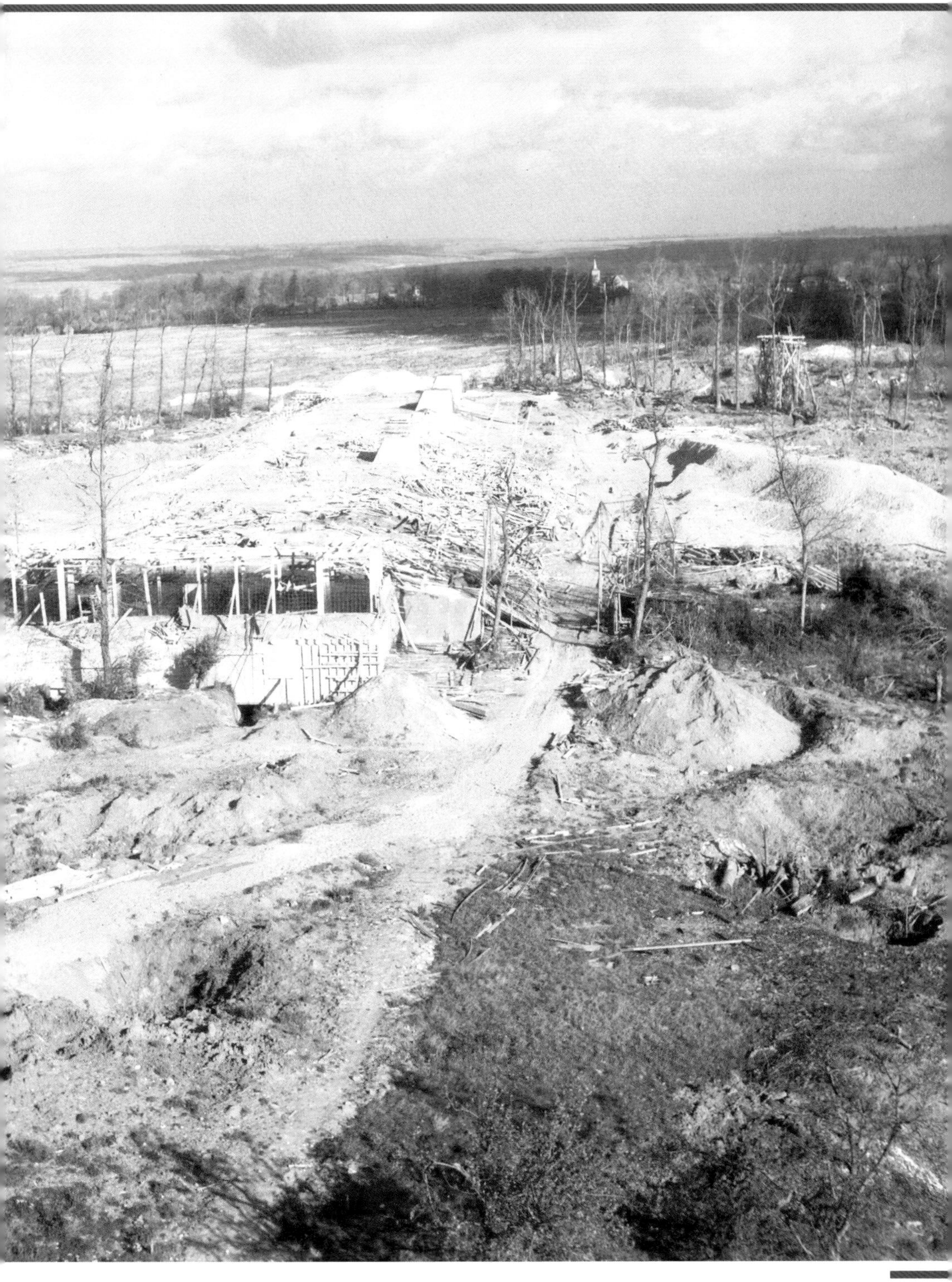

Left: *A vertical, aerial reconnaissance photograph, showing the flying-bomb storage depot at Saint-Leu-d'Esserent, northwest of Paris, France, before the attack by aircraft of Bomber Command on the night of 7/8 July 1944. The weapons were stored in a group of subterranean tunnels formerly used for growing mushrooms.*

Below & Right: *Other aerial photographs, show the damage to the entrances to the subterranean tunnels. The attack was directed by Pathfinder aircraft which accurately marked the approach roads and the mouths of the tunnels in which the flying-bombs were stored. The subsequent bombing not only blocked access to the dump, but caused a landslide which blocked the tunnel entrances too.*

On 4 and 5 July, 617 Squadron used Tallboy bombs in an attempt to collapse the limestone roof of the caves at Saint-Leu-d'Esserent which were being used to store V-1s. The bombing started on 4 July, when 17 Lancasters, 1 Mosquito and 1 Mustang attacked. The second wave came in on 5 July using 1,000lb bombs. Both raids were said to be accurate, but 13 Lancasters were lost to German fighters. Another attack was made on Saint-Leu-d'Esserent by 208 Lancasters and 13 Mosquitoes on the evening of 7 July. This time they successfully blocked the tunnels, though 31 planes were shot down by German night fighters.

On 6 July 210 Lancasters had been airborne over northern France, along with 314 Halifaxes, 26 Mosquitoes and 1 Mustang. They attacked five V-weapon targets. Three hits with Tallboys were claimed, but the post-war bombing analysis indicated no direct hits. There was also an attack on Mimoyecques where a Tallboy hit one of the V-3's shafts, blocking galleries with earth and debris. The V-3 supergun was put out of action, saving London from further damage.

Both ends of the railway tunnel at Rilly La Montagne near Rheims were collapsed by Tallboys dropped by 617 Squadron on 27 July. William Reid VC had already dropped his bomb over the target at 12,000 feet, when he felt his aircraft shudder under the impact of a Tallboy, dropped by another Lancaster 6,000 feet above. The bomb tore through the fuselage, cutting all the control cables and fatally weakening the structure.

Reid gave the order to bail out. While his crew made their escape, the plane went into a dive. This pinned Reid to his seat. He reached overhead and managed to release the escape hatch panel, scrambling out just as the Lancaster broke in two. Breaking his arm in the fall, he was captured by a German patrol and spent the rest of the war in Stalag III-A prisoner-of-war camp at Luckenwalde, west of Berlin.

Above & Right: *Aerial reconnaissance photographs, showing damage to the concrete U-boat shelters at Brest, following two Bomber Command daylight raids. The first was by 10 Avro Lancasters of 617 Squadron on 12 August 1944 and the second on the following day by 13 Lancasters of 617 Squadron, joined by 14 others from 9 Squadron. The target was attacked on both occasions using 12,000lb 'Tallboy' deep-penetration bombs, which left the roof structure heavily damaged and perforated it in at least two places.*

On 5 August, 15 Lancasters of 617 Squadron attacked the U-boat pens at Brest, and scored five direct hits with Tallboys penetrating the concrete roofs. Three penetrated the pens, and the breakwater outside was also damaged. One Lancaster Mark III, piloted by Flying Officer Don Cheney of the Royal Canadian Air Force, was shot down. The plane was hit by flak, severely injuring Flight Sergeant Reginald Pool and Pilot Officer Robert Welsh. Cheney gave the order to bail out of the aircraft. Welsh was shot by the Germans while descending by parachute. Pool's body was found on the shore by the French underground and the body of Pilot Officer William Noel Watt was found in the sea. Cheney and two other crew members managed to survive and were looked after by the French underground. The final crew member was captured by the Germans and sent to a prisoner of war camp. Cheney was awarded the Distinguished Flying Cross (DFC).

Other attacks were made on the submarine bases at Keroman, Lorient, La Rochelle and Ijmuiden in the Netherlands.

On the night of 23 September, Tallboys scored six direct hits on the Dortmund-Ems Canal near Ladbergen, north of Münster. On 7 October, 617 Squadron attacked the Kembe dam north of Basle, to release water that could have been used to flood an area that US troops were about to advance through. Then on 15 October 9 Squadron hit the Sorpe dam with Tallboys, but did not breach it.

Left: Aerial reconnaissance photograph, showing a damaged section of the Dortmund-Ems Canal near Ladbergen, north of Munster, Germany, following a raid by aircraft of No 5 Group, Bomber Command, on the night of 23/24 September 1944. Breaches have been made in the banks of two parallel branches of the canal, causing a six-mile stretch to be drained. Most of the damage was caused by two direct hits by 12,000lb 'Tallboy' deep-penetration bombs dropped by 617 Squadron.

Right: Aerial reconnaissance photograph of the German battleship Tirpitz *moored in Narvik-Bogen Fjord, Norway.*

Below: A low-level aerial photograph taken from a De Havilland Mosquito PR Mark XVI, NS637, of 544 Squadron, showing the capsized German battleship lying in Tromso Fjord off Norway, with a salvage vessel alongside on 22 March 1944.

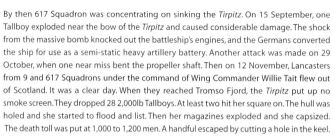

By then 617 Squadron was concentrating on sinking the *Tirpitz*. On 15 September, one Tallboy exploded near the bow of the *Tirpitz* and caused considerable damage. The shock from the massive bomb knocked out the battleship's engines, and the Germans converted the ship for use as a semi-static heavy artillery battery. Another attack was made on 29 October, when one near miss bent the propeller shaft. Then on 12 November, Lancasters from 9 and 617 Squadrons under the command of Wing Commander Willie Tait flew out of Scotland. It was a clear day. When they reached Tromso Fjord, the *Tirpitz* put up no smoke screen. They dropped 28 2,000lb Tallboys. At least two hit her square on. The hull was holed and she started to flood and list. Then her magazines exploded and she capsized. The death toll was put at 1,000 to 1,200 men. A handful escaped by cutting a hole in the keel.

Attacks were made on the Urft dam 30 miles southwest of Cologne on 8 and 11 December 1944, again to stop the Germans flooding areas where Allied troops were going to advance.

The U-boat pens at Ijmuiden were attacked with Tallboys again on 15 December 1944 and 12 January, but smoke obscured the results. So on 3 February 1945 36 Lancasters dropped Tallboys on Ijmuiden and Poortershaven, claiming to have taken out both targets without loss.

Bergen was also hit on 12 January. U-boats had been transferred to Norway after the Germans had withdrawn from France in 1944. A raid had been made on 4 October 1944 by 47 Lancasters, 93 Halifaxes and 12 Mosquitoes. In 11 minutes, they dropped 1,260 992lb bombs and 172 496lb bombs. The Germans lost 12 men and two U-boats. It is thought that a number of Russian prisoners of war working the U-boat pens were also killed. Some 193 Norwegian civilians, including a large number of children, died as a result of the bomb raid, 180 were wounded, 60 houses were totally destroyed and over 700 people were made homeless.

Below: Aerial reconnaissance photograph, taken over the E- and R-Boat pens at Ijmuiden, Holland, following the daylight raid by 17 Avro Lancasters of 617 Squadron, led by their Commanding Officer, Wing Commander J B Tait, on 15 December 1944. Craters ring the target area, and part of the roof over the lower west half of the pen entrances has collapsed as a result of bombs blasting away the division walls. 617 Squadron used 12,000lb deep-penetration 'Tallboy' bombs, one of which has completely perforated the roof, leaving a 15-foot diameter hole.

Above: *A 22,000lb MC, deep-penetration bomb (Bomber Command executive codeword 'Grand Slam') falls away from Avro Lancaster B Mark I (Special), PB996 YZ-C, of 617 Squadron, flown by Flying Officer P Martin and crew, over the viaduct at Arnsberg, Germany.*

In a second raid on 29 October 1944, 244 planes dropped just 47 bombs, due to dense clouds. The 47 bombs killed 52 local civilians and no Germans. No damage was inflicted on the U-boat pens, and three planes were shot down.

But on 12 January the Lancasters were carrying Tallboys. The attack was made by 32 Lancasters and 1 Mosquito of 9 and 617 Squadrons. Three Tallboys penetrated the 10-foot thick roof of the pens and caused severe damage to workshops, offices and stores inside. It has since been repaired and is used to house Norwegian submarines.

The Lancasters were told that, if they could not guarantee a hit on the U-boat pens, they should attack secondary targets such as shipping. One Lancaster saw a minesweeper heading out of Bergen harbour and attacked it. The bomber scored a direct hit with its Tallboy, killing 20 of the crew.

Left: Aerial reconnaissance photograph of the 'Hoheitsgebiet' – containing Adolf Hitler's chalet and SS guard barracks – at Obersalzburg near Berchtesgaden, Germany. This was taken prior to the daylight attack by aircraft of Bomber Command on 25 April 1944. Principal buildings include the SS barracks, training hall and garages (top), the Platterhof garage and servants' quarters and Platterhof Pension (centre right), Hitler's guest house (bottom) Hitler's chalet, the Berghof (left), and immediately above it, the offices of the Security Service (formerly 'Gasthof zum Tuerken'). Above this at upper left is Martin Bormann's house.

Below: Vertical aerial photograph taken during the daylight raid on Adolf Hitler's chalet complex and the SS guard barracks by 359 Avro Lancasters and 16 De Havilland Mosquitos of Nos 1, 5 and 8 Groups. The SS barracks are at upper left, partly obscured by smoke from the attack. Hitler's chalet, the Berghof, is at lower centre, and the Platterhof Pension and Hitler's guest house are on the right. The bombing was reported to be accurate and effective.

Three Lancasters of 617 Squadron and one from 9 Squadron were lost. One plane from 617 Squadron was attacked by German Me190s off the Norwegian coast. A Lancaster's engine caught fire, but it made a perfect landing on the sea. All the crew were seen to scramble on top of the aircraft and life-saving equipment was dropped to them by a Warwick aircraft. However, a Junkers 88 strafed the downed Lancaster, killing the survivors. Only one body was found – that of Flying Officer Mowbray Ellwood, who is buried in the cemetery in Trondheim.

While the first Grand Slam had just been used to take out the Bielefeld viaduct on 14 March 1945, more Tallboys were being dropped on the Arnsberg viaduct. It was attacked again the following day, but still did not collapse. Then on 19 March, 37 Lancasters attacked the railway viaduct at Arnsberg and the bridge at Vlotho, near Minden. The attack at Arnsberg was made by 617 Squadron, using six Grand Slams. This time they blew a 40-foot gap in the viaduct. However, 9 Squadron's attack on Vlotho was not successful.

Grand Slams were used again for an attack on the Valentin submarine pens at Farge near Bremen. These had a roof made of ferrous concrete up to 23-feet thick. Two Grand Slam bombs penetrated a section just 15-feet thick and detonated, rendering the shelter unusable. No aircraft were lost in the raid.

Both Tallboys and Grand Slams were used for an attack by 17 Lancasters on Hamburg on 9 April. Some of the bombs hit their targets and no aircraft were lost.

Below: *Operation Manna. Ground crew loading food supplies into slings for hoisting into the bomb bay of an Avro Lancaster of 514 Squadron at Waterbeach, Cambridgeshire. Between 29 April and 7 May 1945, Lancasters of Bomber Command dropped 6,672 tons of food to the starving populace of a large area in western Holland still in German hands.*

The pocket battleship *Lützow* was attacked on 16 April by 617 Squadron. Despite intense flak, 18 aircraft managed to bomb the target – 14 carrying Tallboys and 4 carrying 1,000lb bombs. One near miss with a Tallboy tore a large hole in the bottom of the *Lützow* and she settled to the bottom in shallow water. One Lancaster was shot down. It was to be 617 Squadron's last loss in the war.

On 19 April, 617 Lancasters, supported by 332 Halifaxes and 20 Mosquitoes, dropped Tallboys on the naval base, airfield and town on Heligoland. Three Halifaxes were lost and the islands were evacuated the following night.

The last Lancaster operation in Germany came on 25 April. Fittingly, it was an attack on Hitler's Bavarian holiday home, the Berghof, near Berchtesgaden. A mixed force which included six Lancasters of 617 Squadron, dropping their last Tallboys, destroyed an SS barracks.

Below: Liberated prisoners of war walk out to Lancaster bombers at Lübeck Aerodrome, Germany, waiting to fly them home to Britain – 11 May 1945.

By the end of the war, 56 squadrons of Bomber Command were equipped with the Lancaster. Three bomber groups were entirely composed of Lancasters. The Pathfinders used it as their sole heavy bomber. A fourth bomber group was also converting from Halifaxes and, if the war had gone on longer, it is thought that the Halifax would have been phased out entirely in favour of the Lanc.

In the last days of the war in Europe, Lancasters were used to drop food supplies to the Netherlands where the liberated populace were starving. Most Bomber Command squadrons were then moved to Transport Command and played an important role in transporting liberated prisoners of war back to Britain. Lancasters from Bomber Command were then to have formed the main strength of Tiger Force. This was to have been the Commonwealth bomber contingent flying from bases on Okinawa that were to have taken part in Operation Downfall, the codename for the planned invasion of Japan, scheduled for the end of 1945. By then though, the war in the Far East had been terminated by the dropping of the atomic bomb.

Bomber Command phased out the Lancaster between 1946 and 1950, in favour of the Avro Lincoln, originally developed as the Lancaster Mark IV and V. In 1946, four Lancasters were converted by Avro for use by British South American Airways, but they proved to be uneconomical and were withdrawn after a year in service.

Four Lancaster Mark IIIs were converted for in-flight refuelling. In 1947, one was flown non-stop 3,355 miles from London to Bermuda. Later the two tanker aircraft were joined by another converted Lancaster and were used in the Berlin airlift, making 757 tanker sorties.

The last Lancaster actually in service with the RAF was used by Fighter Command as a photographic aircraft. It retired in late 1954. However, Lancasters sold on to Argentina saw service in a number of military coups.

William Reid VC

William Reid was a 21-year-old Acting Flight Lieutenant flying Lancasters with 61 Squadron when he took part in the raid on Düsseldorf in Germany on the night of 3 November 1943. On the way to the target, his windscreen was shattered by gun fire from a Messerschmitt. The cockpit and the gun turrets were also badly damaged. Although he was injured and his plane damaged, he continued on his mission. Soon afterwards the bomber was attacked again. His navigator was killed and the wireless operator fatally wounded. Reid was wounded again, along with the flight engineer, and the Lancaster received more serious damage. Nevertheless, he continued to his target, dropped his bombs and turned for home.

On the way back to RAF Syerston, near Newark, he saw the searchlights of RAF Shipdham, a USAAF-operated base in Norfolk. Although he was suffering from loss of blood, he managed to put the plane down. As it hit the runway, the undercarriage collapsed on landing and the Lancaster slid to a halt. The wireless operator died in Shipdham's medical centre, but the rest of the crew survived.

Norman Jackson VC

Sergeant Norman Jackson completed his tour of 30 missions, but on the night of 26 April 1944 he volunteered to make one more sortie. The target was a ball-bearing factory at Schweinfurt. Having bombed the target, Jackson's Lancaster was attacked by a German night fighter and a fuel tank in the starboard wing caught fire. Already wounded from shell splinters, Sergeant Jackson, the flight engineer, grabbed a fire extinguisher and jettisoned the escape hatch above the pilot's head. He then started to climb out of the cockpit and back along the top of the fuselage towards the starboard wing. Before he could leave the fuselage his parachute pack opened and the whole canopy and rigging lines spilled into the cockpit. Undeterred, Sergeant Jackson continued. The pilot, bomb aimer and navigator gathered the parachute together and held on to the rigging lines, paying them out as the airman crawled aft. Eventually he slipped and, falling from the fuselage to the starboard wing, grasped an air intake on the leading edge of the wing. He succeeded in clinging on, but lost the extinguisher.

By this time, the fire had spread. Sergeant Jackson's face, hands and clothing were severely burnt. Unable to retain his grip, he was swept through the flames and over the trailing edge of the wing, dragging his parachute behind him. Having already sustained serious injuries, he fell 20,000 feet to the ground. His parachute was burnt and only partially opened. Unable to control his descent, he landed heavily and broke an ankle. His right eye was closed and his hands were useless. At daybreak he crawled to the nearest village, where he was taken prisoner. After ten months in hospital he made a good recovery, though his hands required further treatment and were only of limited use. He was then transferred to a prisoner of war camp.

After he returned home, he received his Victoria Cross in person from King George VI at Buckingham Palace on 13 November 1945. The citation pointed out: "To venture outside, when travelling at 200 miles an hour, at a great height and in intense cold, was an almost incredible feat. Had he succeeded in subduing the flames, there was little or no prospect of his regaining the cockpit."

Jackson was promoted to Warrant Officer. He died in 1994. In 2004, his Victoria Cross fetched £200,000 at auction.

Robert Palmer VC

On 23 December 1944, 24-year-old Squadron Leader Robert Palmer was leading a formation of Lancaster bombers making a daylight raid on the marshalling yards at Cologne. It was his 110th mission. Some minutes before reaching the target he came under heavy anti-aircraft fire. Two engines caught fire, but he continued. Determined to provide a clear aiming point for the other bombers, he managed to keep the badly damaged aircraft on a straight course. He made a perfect approach and released his bombs. His Lancaster was last seen spiralling to earth in flames. His remains were buried at Rheinberg War Cemetery in Germany.

George Thompson VC

On 1 January 1945, 24-year-old Flight Sergeant George Thompson was the wireless operator on board a Lancaster attacking the Dortmund-Ems Canal. After releasing its bombs, the plane was hit by flak that tore holes in the fuselage and started several fires. Thompson saw that the mid-upper turret was ablaze. The gunner inside was unconscious. At the cost of severe burns to his hands and face Thompson managed to reach the gunner and carry him clear. The rear turret was on fire too and its gunner had also been overcome by fumes. Although his hands were already burnt, Thompson beat out the flames on the rear gunner's clothing and pulled him clear. Then he made his way forward, edging round a hole in the flooring, to tell his captain what was happening. Despite much damage to the aircraft and a fire in one engine, the pilot managed to reach Belgium and successfully crash-landed. Thompson and one of the gunners died later from their injuries.

Leonard Cheshire VC

In July 1944, Captain Leonard Cheshire completed his 100th operation. He had led 617 Squadron on a 'large site' at Mimoyecques, which turned out to be the shelter for Hitler's V-3. Then his commanding officer, Air Vice-Marshal Ralph Cochrane, took him off operations. In September 1944, he was awarded the Victoria Cross, not for any one action but for his whole career as a bomber pilot.

Right: The strain of command and operational flying is apparent on the faces of Group Captain Percy Pickard DSO and Bar, DFC (left), Squadron Leader William Blessing DSO, DFC, RAAF, and Group Captain Geoffrey Leonard Cheshire (right) DSO and Bar, DFC, at an investiture at Buckingham Palace, 28 July 1943.

Edwin Swales VC

Captain Edwin Swales was master bomber of a force of Lancasters that attacked Pforzheim on the night of 23 February 1945. Soon after he reached the target area he was attacked by an enemy fighter and one of his engines was put out of action. His rear guns failed and his crippled aircraft was an easy prey for further attacks. Undeterred, he carried on issuing aiming instructions to the main force. The enemy fighter closed again and the second engine of Captain Swales' aircraft was put out of action. Now practically defenceless, he stayed over the target area, issuing his aiming instructions and making the attack one of the most concentrated and successful of the war.

Captain Swales turned for home, though the plane's speed had been reduced so much that it was difficult to keep it in the air and the blind-flying instruments were no longer working. He was determined to prevent his aircraft and crew from falling into enemy hands. After an hour he flew into thin-layered cloud. He kept his course by skilful flying between the layers. Then he met heavy cloud and turbulent air conditions. Now over friendly territory, the aircraft became more difficult to control and was losing height steadily. Swales ordered his crew to bail out. When the last crew member had jumped, the aircraft plunged to earth. Swales was found dead at the controls.

Below: The Lancaster 1, second prototype, with Rolls-Royce Merlin XX engines, seen here in August 1942.

Chapter Nine

Variants

The original Mark I Lancaster was powered by Rolls-Royce Merlin XX engines and SU carburettors. Minor details were changed throughout the production series. The pitot head for measuring airspeed was originally on a long mast at the front of the nose. It was later moved to a short fairing mounted on the side of the fuselage under the cockpit. Other minor changes had to be made to accommodate the latest radar equipment. Later production Lancasters had Merlin 22 and 24 engines, but no major design changes were needed to accommodate these engines.

Below: A Rolls-Royce Merlin XX engine, seen from the port side and a picture showing a Rolls-Royce Merlin 24 engine (bottom), fitted to the Lancaster, 'Just Jane' (below) that is now kept at the Lincolnshire Aviation Heritage Centre in East Kirkby.

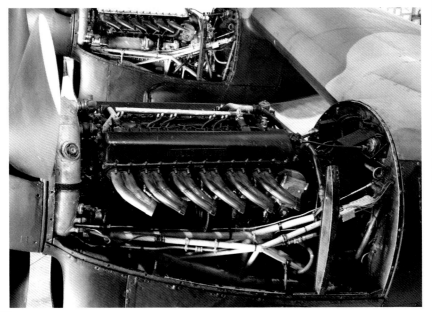

Two special versions of the Mark I Lancasters were developed during the war. The first was the Mark I Special designed for 617 Squadron to carry Barnes Wallis's bouncing bomb. Nineteen Lancasters had their bomb-bay doors removed. Struts built by Vickers were fitted in their place to carry the bomb. The dorsal turret was removed to save weight and a hydraulic motor, driven by the pump previously used for the dorsal turret, was fitted to spin the bomb. Spot lamps were fitted in the bomb bay and nose for the simple height measurement system needed for low-flying at night. Although the dorsal gunner was no longer needed, the seven-man crew was retained and he was moved to the front turret to man the guns there, so the bomb aimer could concentrate on assisting the navigator with map reading. During the Dambusters raids, 8 of the 19 Mark I Specials were lost. The remaining aircraft were restored to standard specifications.

Below: *An Avro Lancaster B Mark I Special of 617 Squadron, loaded with a 22,000lb MC deep-penetration bomb 'Grand Slam', running an engine test in its dispersal at Woodhall Spa, Lincolnshire, England.*

The other Mark I Special was adapted to take first the heavy Tallboy bomb and then the super-heavy Grand Slam. Upgraded Mark 24 Merlin engines with paddle-bladed propellers were used to give more power. To take the Tallboy, the bomb-bay doors were adapted to bulge outwards. For the Grand Slam, they were removed completely. Fairings were used to reduce the drag. On some Tallboy raids, the dorsal turret was removed. This modification was retained for the Grand Slam aircraft. Later the nose turret and two guns from the rear turret were also removed.

Two airframes were modified to carry a dorsal saddle tank. They were mounted aft of a modified canopy and carried 1,200 gallons of fuel for increased range. The aircraft were flight tested in India and Australia in 1945 when it was planned to use the Lancaster in the final phase of the Pacific war. However, when full, the saddle tank made handling difficult and, when greater range was required, in-flight refuelling was used instead.

Another version of the Mark I was developed for use in the Far East. The Mark I (FE) carried an extra 400 gallons of fuel in the bomb bay. It was modified for tropical conditions and, for long flights over the Pacific, it was equipped with the latest upgraded navigation, radio and radar equipment. The dorsal turret was also removed. The Mark I (FE) was intended to make up the British component of Tiger Force being assembled on Okinawa, ready to invade Japan. However, the war in the Pacific ended before any reached the Far East.

There was also a photographic reconnaissance version of the Mark I, operated during the war by 82 and 541 Squadrons. All armament and turrets were removed. The nose was reconfigured and a camera was carried in the bomb bay. From around 1950, 683 Squadron used the PR I for photographic reconnaissance from its base in Aden, and subsequently, from Habbaniya in Iraq until the unit was disbanded in November 1953.

The Mark II was the only version of the Lancaster not to be powered by Merlin engines. Instead, it used Bristol Hercules VI or XVI radial air-cooled engines. One difference between the two engine versions was that the VI had a manual mixture control that required an extra lever on the throttle pedestal.

Above: Lancaster Mark II, DS604 QR-W, of
61 Squadron, on the ground at Syerston,
Nottinghamshire. DS604 later joined
115 Squadron and was lost over Frankfurt
on 10/11 April 1943.

Left: Avro Lancaster B Mark II, LL725
EQ-C, of 408 Squadron Royal Canadian
Air Force (RCAF), on the ground at Linton-
on-Ouse, Yorkshire. Armourers are
backing a tractor and trolley loaded
with a 4,000lb HE bomb, 'cookie', and
incendiaries under the open bomb-bay.
LL725 was lost over Hamburg on
28/29 July 1944.

The Mark II was intended as a stopgap, so that Lancasters could still be produced if the supply of Merlin engines faltered. British production was vulnerable to German bombing and there were worries that the American engines produced by Packard would be diverted or stopped if America entered the war. Merlin engines also powered the Spitfire and Hurricane and the production of fighters was given a higher priority at that time.

Work on the prototype Mark II began soon after the Mark I was completed. The first prototype flew on 26 November 1941. Production models were almost always fitted with an FN64 ventral turret and had a pronounced step in the bulged bomb bay. The Mark II was produced by Armstrong Whitworth who began production in March 1942. But while Rolls-Royce was free from serious air attack, the Armstrong Whitworth factory was bombed in June 1942, delaying the appearance of the new model.

Below: Lancaster B Mark II, DS652 KO-B, of 115 Squadron, undergoing a test of its Bristol Hercules V, sleeve-valve, radial engines in a dispersal at East Wretham, Norfolk. DS652 failed to return from a raid on Bochum, Germany, on 12/13 June 1943.

By the time the Mark II entered service in October 1942, the threat to Merlin production was already receding. Initial service tests with 61 Squadron early in 1943 then revealed a serious limitation. The Mark II had an unexpectedly low service ceiling. When two Mark IIs joined a formation of Mark Is attacking Essen on the night of 11 January 1943, while the Mark Is operated at 22,000 feet, one Mark II could only reach 18,400 feet, the other just 14,000 feet.

After the tests were finished, 115 Squadron were equipped with Mark II Lancasters. Despite its low ceiling, the Mark II was still a welcome improvement on the Wellingtons they had been flying before. In service, the Mark II proved more robust than the Mark I. Its air-cooled Bristol engine did not have the Merlin's vulnerable liquid cooling system. The ventral turret also improved its chances of survival, although it was sometimes removed to save weight. However, flying at a lower altitude, the Mark II was more vulnerable to flak.

A second problem was that the Mark II could only carry 14,000lb of bombs, compared to the Mark I's bomb load of 18,000lb. Generally, the Hercules-powered Lancaster Mark II had an all-round performance comparable to the Merlin XX powered Halifax Mark II. Some 300 Lancaster Mark IIs were made, but by the end of 1943 they were being phased out. Armstrong Whitworth switched to production of the Mark I as there had been no interruption to the production of Merlin engines. Indeed, the supply of engines by Packard increased after America entered the war. At the same time, Handley Page had turned to the Hercules engine to power their Mark III Halifax, ironically improving the plane's performance.

By D-Day, only 514 and 408 Squadrons were still using Lancaster Mark IIs. All other squadrons had either Lancaster Mark Is or Mark IIIs or Halifax Mark IIIs. A small number of Mark IIs remained in use as test beds. The last survived until 1950.

Below: *The bomb load most commonly used for area bombing raids (Bomber Command executive codeword 'Usual') in the bomb bay of an Avro Lancaster of 57 Squadron at Scampton Lincolnshire. 'Usual' consisted of a 4,000lb impact-fused HC bomb ('cookie'), and 12 Small Bomb Containers (SBCs) each loaded with incendiaries, in this case 236 4lb incendiary sticks.*

The Mark III Lancaster was produced at the same time as the Mark I. The two planes were externally identical. But while the Mark I had a Merlin engine built in Britain by Rolls-Royce, the Mark III's engines were built under licence by Packard in the United States. There were minor differences due to the different engines. For example, the Packard engines had a Bendix Stromberg pressure-injection carburettor which needed slow-running cut-off switches in the cockpit. The Packard Merlin 28, capable of delivering 1,420 horsepower at take-off, was also slightly more likely to overheat during take-off and landing, making the plane less suitable for use in training units.

Some 3,039 Mark IIIs were built, almost all at A V Roe's Newton Heath factory. As with the Mark I, minor modifications were made as new batches were ordered. These included the relocation of the pitot head from the nose to the side of the cockpit, and the change from de Havilland 'needle blade' propellers to Hamilton Standard or Nash Kelvinator made 'paddle blade' propellers. A number of Mark III Specials were also made. These were standard Mark IIIs modified for use on the Dambusters raid.

Mark IIIs were also modified for maritime reconnaissance and air-sea rescue. The armament was usually removed and the dorsal turret taken out, especially in post-war use. Observation windows were installed on both sides of the rear fuselage. The starboard window was added to the rear access door, while the port window was just forward of the tailplane. Three dipole antennas were fitted under the plane behind the radome to improve communication. For air-sea rescue, a lifeboat was carried in the re-configured bomb bay, which was dropped by the bomb aimer.

Below: Lancaster B Mark VI, JB675 at Hucknall, Nottinghamshire, after conversion from a B Mark III by Rolls-Royce Ltd, who installed 1,635hp Merlin 85 engines and four-bladed propellers. Following performance trials at the Aeroplane and Armament Experimental Establishment, JB675 served a lengthy period of operational trials with 7, 405, 635 and 76 Squadrons of the RAF before retirement to the Royal Aircraft Establishment.

Above: *Avro Lancaster B Mark III, ED724 PM-M, of 103 Squadron, pauses on the flarepath at Elsham Wolds, Lincolnshire, England, before taking off for a raid on Duisburg, Germany, during the Battle of the Ruhr. Three searchlights (called 'Sandra' lights) form a cone to indicate the height of the cloud base for the departing aircraft.*

The Mark IV had a longer fuselage and increased wingspan. It had a new Boulton Paul F turret with two 0.5-inch machine guns and re-configured, framed 'bay window' nose glazing. The three prototypes were powered by Merlin 68s outboard and Merlin 85s inboard. Merlin 85s had two-stage superchargers which gave improved performance at high altitude. These prototypes became the basis of the Lincoln Mark I bomber, while the Mark V became the Lincoln Mark II.

Nine Lancaster Mark IIIs were converted to use the Merlin 85 and 87 engines, becoming the Lancaster Mark VI. This did not enter mass production, because the Merlin 85 only produced 1,635 horsepower, just 25 horsepower more than the Merlin 24 used in late-production Lancaster Mark Is. However, they did have improved altitude performance, especially when the nose and dorsal turrets were removed and faired over. Late in 1944, five of the Mark VIs served with the Pathfinder squadrons, usually as the 'master bomber' who commanded the raid.

Below: The first Canadian-built Avro Lancaster B Mark X, KB700
'The Ruhr Express', taxiing after landing at Northolt, Middlesex, following a
delivery flight across the Atlantic. KB700 was the first of 300 aircraft built by
Victory Aircraft of Malton, Ontario, and flew operationally with 405 and 419
Squadrons of the Royal Canadian Air Force (RCAF).

The Mark VII was the final production version of the Lancaster. It was made by Austin at their Longbridge factory. The main difference between the Mark VII and late production Mark Is or Mark IIIs was the use of the American-built Martin 250CE turret in place of the Nash & Thomson FN50 dorsal turret. The Martin turret carried two 0.5-inch Browning Mark II machine guns, which packed much more punch than the .303s of the older turret. The heavier Martin turret was also mounted further forward to maintain centre of gravity balance. It was above the bomb bay rather than behind it.

The Martin turret arrived too late for inclusion on the first 50 aircraft built at Longbridge. These retained the FN50 and were officially still Mark Is, though they were often known as the Mark VII (Interim). Some saw service in Europe before the defeat of Germany. Another 180 true Mark VIIs were built. These had the Martin mid-upper turret, along with the Nash & Thomson FN82 rear turret, which also carried two 0.5-inch Brownings, instead of the four 0.303s of the FN20. Both versions were powered by the Merlin 24 engine.

The true Mark VIIs came off the production line too late for the war in Europe. They were then tropicalized and upgraded as the Mark VII (FE) for use in the Far East. Although they were not needed for the invasion of Japan, most did see service overseas.

The Mark X was a Canadian-built Mark III with Canadian- and US-made instrumentation and electrics, and a Packard engine. Built at Victory Aircraft in Malton, Ontario, the early Mark Xs used the Packard Merlin 38, which developed 1,390 horsepower, before moving to the Merlin 224, which gave 1,610 horsepower.

Once the early Mark Xs were airworthy, they were flown to England where the Nash & Thomson gun turrets were fitted. On later batches the FN50 dorsal turret was replaced by the heavier Martin 250CE, which could be installed in Canada. The British H2S downward-looking radar was still added in England.

Above: A 57 Squadron mid-upper gunner scans the sky for enemy aircraft from a Lancaster's Fraser Nash FN50 turret.

Above: Lancaster B Mark X, KB783, at Boscombe Down, Wiltshire. KB783 was fitted with a Martin dorsal turret, and served with 428 and 419 Squadrons of the Royal Canadian Air Force (RCAF) until June 1945.

Some 430 Mark Xs were delivered between September 1943 and March 1945. They were used by 6 (Canadian) Group when it switched from Halifaxes. In May 1945, the surviving Mark Xs returned to Canada in preparation for the expected invasion of Japan.

The Mark X remained in service with the Royal Canadian Air Force for 20 years, serving in a variety of roles including search and rescue, photo-reconnaissance, maritime patrol and jet engine research. The last flight of an RCAF Mark X was at the Calgary International Air Show on 4 July 1964.

Above: Hoisting the final bomb into the bomb-bay of an Avro Lincoln of 57 Squadron, at RAF Tengah, Singapore, prior to an airstrike against insurgents in Malaya.

Avro Lincoln

The Lincoln was Roy Chadwick's development of the Lancaster, built to the Air Ministry Specification B.14/43. The prototype Lincoln was assembled at Manchester's Ringway Airport and made its maiden flight from there on 9 June 1944. It had a longer wingspan and bigger fuselage that could carry more fuel and bigger bomb loads. Initially known as the Lancaster IV and V – with Merlin 68 and Merlin 85 engines – they were redesignated Lincoln I and II.

They became operational too late to be used in World War II. However, some 600 were built to equip 29 RAF squadrons. The RAF's last piston-engined bomber, it was phased out from the late 1950s, and completely replaced by jet-powered bombers by 1963.

The Lincoln saw combat in Kenya during the Mau-Mau insurrection, and Malaya during the Malayan Emergency. A converted Lincoln freighter was used during the Berlin airlift and, on 12 March 1953, a Lincoln Mark II on its way to Berlin on a training flight was shot down by a Soviet MiG-15, killing its crew of seven.

The Royal Australian Air Force employed Lincolns, and 73 were built there between 1946 and 1949. During the 1950s, the RAAF heavily modified some Lincolns for use in anti-submarine warfare.

The Lincoln had a crew of seven and could carry a useful load of 14,000lb. It was 78 feet 3 inches long with a wingspan of 120 feet. It had a top speed of 295mph and a range of 2,930 miles. Its service ceiling was 30,500 feet and its rate of climb was 800 feet a minute.

The Mark III version of the plane became the Avro Shackleton.

Left: Shackleton WR 963, seen here, first flew in march of 1954. It was allocated to 224 Squadron and delivered to Gibraltar in october of the same year. At the end of its service career it was privately purchased and transferred to Coventry Airport, England, in 1991.

Avro Shackleton

The Avro Shackleton was a further development of Roy Chadwick's design for the Lancaster bomber. The design took the Lincoln's wings and landing gear and mated them with a new fuselage. The engines were Rolls-Royce Griffons with 13-foot contra-rotating propellers, creating a distinctive engine noise and adding high-tone deafness to the hazards of the pilots. Initially intended for air-sea rescue, it was known as the Lincoln ASR.3 during development.

The first test flight was in March 1949. Front-line aircraft were delivered to Coastal Command in April 1951 for use in anti-submarine warfare, maritime reconnaissance, airborne early warning and search and rescue. The Shackleton had its operational debut during the Suez Crisis. It remained in service with the RAF until 1990.

The Shackleton carried a crew of ten. It was 87 feet 4 inches long and had a wingspan of 120 feet. Carrying 4,258 gallons of fuel, it had a range of 2,250 miles and could stay airborne for 14 hours 36 minutes. Its service ceiling was 20,200 feet and its top speed was 300mph.

Right: Shackleton 1722, seen here in flight, belonged to the South African Air Force (SAAF). At the end of its service, and after much restoration, it was based at Ysterplaat Air Force Base in Cape Town, South Africa.

Chapter Ten

Surviving Planes

There are some 17 largely complete Avro Lancasters known in the world. Only two are airworthy – one in Britain, one in Canada. The British one is the Mark I Lancaster PA474 'City of Lincoln', that has been operated by the Battle of Britain Memorial Flight since 1973. She was built in Chester in 1945 and earmarked for the Tiger Force in the Far East. As the war with Japan ended before she saw action, she was assigned to photographic reconnaissance duties with 82 Squadron in East and South Africa. Her turrets were removed and she carried the identification letter 'M'.

When she returned to Britain, she was loaned to the company Flight Refuelling Ltd to be used as a pilotless drone. Before the conversion started, the Air Ministry decided to use a Lincoln instead and PA474 was sent to the Royal College of Aeronautics, where she was used for trials of experimental wings: trial wings were mounted vertically on the top of the rear fuselage.

Right: PA474 is one of the remaining Lancasters that can actually fly, and it makes up part of the Battle of Britain Memorial Flight (BBMF) collection. From 2000 the aircraft was painted in the markings originally worn by Lancaster III EE176 QR-M ('Mickey the Moocher') of 61 Squadron, based at Skellingthorpe. On the 2 October 2006 she made her last flight in these colours and was delivered to Air Atlantique at Coventry for a major service, before joining the BBMF.

In 1964, PA474 was adopted by the Air Historical Branch for future display in the proposed RAF Museum at Hendon. She was flown to Wroughton where she was painted in a camouflage paint scheme. She then took part in two films – *The Guns of Navarone* and *Operation Crossbow*. Later that year she was transferred to RAF Henlow to be prepared for the RAF Museum.

However, there was a prior claim. The first unit to be equipped with Lancasters in 1941 was 44 Squadron. In 1965, the Commanding Officer of the unit, now flying Vulcans from RAF Waddington, asked for PA474 to be transferred to the care of the squadron. As the plane was still structurally sound, it was given permission to make a single flight from Henlow to Waddington. At Waddington, PA474 underwent an extensive restoration programme. Both her front and rear turrets were replaced. Then in 1967, the plane was given permission to fly regularly, though restoration work has continued ever since.

In November 1973, PA474 joined the Battle of Britain Flight, which then changed its name to the Battle of Britain Memorial Flight. In 1975, a dorsal turret was found in Argentina. This was shipped to England on board HMS *Hampshire* and fitted to PA474. That same year the aircraft was officially adopted by the City of Lincoln.

During the winter of 1995 she was given a new main spar, extending her life for the foreseeable future. Then in the winter of 2006, she was given a major servicing at Air Atlantique in Coventry. Her paint scheme is changed periodically to represent notable Lancasters. She currently wears the markings of EE139, the 'Phantom of the Ruhr', a Lancaster that survived over 100 operations. EE139 flew her first 30 operations with 100 Squadron based at Waltham, before completing another 91 sorties with 550 Squadron at North Killingholme. Consequently, PA474 – masquerading as EE139 – carries her 100 Squadron identification letters, HR-W, on her port side and the BQ-B of 550 Squadron on her starboard side.

Left: *PA474 in full flight. There is something very special in seeing one of these rare machines in flight, and hearing the sound of the four Merlin engines is enough to send a shiver down your back.*

Canada's airworthy Lancaster is FM213, a Mark X. She was part of the second batch of 130 aircraft produced by Victory Aircraft Ltd of Malton, Ontario. They were equipped with Packard-built Merlin 22, 38 or 224 engines. The serial numbers of this batch run from FM100 to FM229. Four other planes from this batch have survived, along with parts of two others.

She was converted for maritime reconnaissance and later served with an air-sea rescue unit. When she was retired from service by the RCAF on 6 November 1963, she had a staggering 4,392.3 hours on the airframe. She went into storage in Dunnville, Ontario, and would probably have been sold for scrap if it had not been for the intervention of the Royal Canadian Legion in Goderich. She was restored to flying condition by the Canadian Warplane Heritage Museum in 1988. The aircraft is flown in the paint scheme of KB726 VR-A, and is known as the 'Mynarski Memorial Lancaster' in honour of Canadian Victoria Cross winner Andrew Mynarski who flew the original. The museum offers guided tours of the interior by appointment.

Below & left: *The Canadian Warplane Heritage Museum is the patron of the second of only two Lancasters in the world that can still fly. It is located at Airport Road, Mount Hope, at the Hamilton International Airport in Canada. The CWH Museum has dedicated its Lancaster to the memory of Pilot Officer Andrew Charles Mynarski, VC, of 419 (Moose) Squadron, 6 (RCAF) Group. Mynarski won the only Victoria Cross for 6 Group, the Commonwealth's highest award for gallantry in battle. On the night of 12/13 June 1944, his Lancaster X was shot down by a Luftwaffe night fighter. As it started its plunge towards the ground, Mynarski, his flying clothing already in flames, tried in vain to free his trapped rear gunner from the jammed rear turret. Miraculously, the gunner lived to relate the story of Mynarski's bravery, but sadly Mynarski himself died from his severe burns.*

Above: The crew of the first Lancaster to reach
Australia, ED 930 'Queenie', with their aircraft at
Prestwick in May 1943, before setting off on its
record-breaking 72-hour flight via Canada
and the USA.

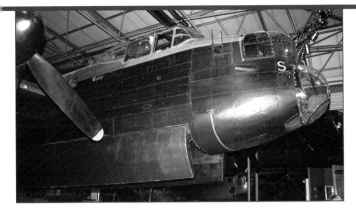

Left: *After being returned to her wartime configuration, R5868 can be seen in one of the large hangars at the RAF Museum, Hendon, London.*

Four more Lancasters that served with Bomber Command in the campaign over Europe have survived, but none of them are airworthy.

Below: *The veteran Avro Lancaster bomber 'S for Sugar', of 467 Squadron, Royal Australian Air Force (RAAF), is prepared for its 97th operational sortie at RAF Waddington, Lincolnshire.*

Lancaster R5868 is the oldest surviving Lancaster. She was part of the first production batch of 57 Manchester Bomber aircraft ordered from Metropolitan-Vickers Ltd in Trafford Park, Manchester, and built at the Mosley Road Works. All 57 aircraft were converted to Lancaster Mark Is on the production line. The serial numbers of this batch included R5842–R5860 and R5888–R5917. Deliveries started in January 1942 and finished in September 1942, with bombers leaving the production line at an average rate of seven aircraft a week.

She flew 137 operations, originally as 'Q-Queenie' with the RAF's 83 Squadron based at RAF Scampton, then as 'S-Sugar' with 463 and 467 RAAF Squadrons from RAF Waddington. She was the first RAF heavy bomber to complete 100 operations. Returned to her wartime configuration, she is now on display at the RAF Museum in Hendon.

Another surviving Mark I, W4783, was part of the second production batch of 200 aircraft ordered from Metropolitan-Vickers Ltd in Trafford Park and built at the Mosley Road Works. The first 170 aircraft were delivered as Mark Is with serial numbers W4761–W4800, W4815–W4864, W4879–W4905, W4918–4967 and W4980–W4982. The remaining 30 aircraft were delivered as Mark IIIs using American-built Packard Merlin engines and had serial numbers between W4983 and W5012. Deliveries began September 1942 and finished May 1943, but the average rate of production had dropped to six aircraft per week.

W4783 operated as 'G-George' and flew with 460 Squadron RAAF. After completing 90 sorties, she was flown to Australia during the war for fundraising purposes. There she was assigned the Australian serial number A66-2. She later went on display at the Australian War Memorial in Canberra, and underwent a thorough restoration between 1999 and 2003.

Part of another Mark I from that batch also survives. W4964 flew as 'WS-J' with 9 Squadron and completed 109 sorties before becoming ground instruction machine 4922M in December 1944. Remains of W4964's mid-fuselage section are on public display at the Newark Air Museum in Nottinghamshire.

KB839 was part of the first production batch of 300 aircraft ordered from Victory Aircraft Ltd, who delivered them at a rate of four a week. The serial numbers of that batch run from KB700 to KB999. The first 75 had the Packard-built Merlin 38 engines; the remaining 225 aircraft got the Packard Merlin 224. Five of this batch survive, along with parts of two others.

Right: The Greenwood Military Aviation Museum in Greenwood, Nova Scotia, Canada, looks after Lancaster X, KB839, which was built in 1945 at Victory Aircraft Ltd, Malton, Ontario.

The first of these planes was sent to England in September 1943, the last in May 1945. KB839 was delivered to 419 Squadron RCAF in January 1945. Wearing the code letters 'VR-D', she completed 26 sorties. After the end of the war in Europe, she was returned to Canada where she was modified for aerial reconnaissance with 408 'Goose' Squadron based at RCAF Station Rockcliffe, Ontario. She is now preserved at the Greenwood Military Aviation Museum in Nova Scotia, where she is currently on display.

Left: Lancaster W4783/AR-G, 'G-George' of 460 Squadron, RAAF, was delivered in October 1942 and went on to complete 90 operations. It is seen here running up its engines at Prestwick on 11 October 1944, before setting out on its long retirement journey to Australia, where it was to be preserved as a memorial to the Australians of Bomber Command.

Below: The Lincolnshire Aviation Heritage Centre in East Kirby, Lincolnshire, is the home of Avro Lancaster Mk VII, NX611 'Just Jane'. Although this aircraft is not airworthy, you can still take a ride in it along the old runway. Just being inside this aircraft, hearing the incredible noise of those 4 Merlin engines and feeling the excitement of taxiing along the runway can be a wonderful, and, to many, an emotional, thrill.

KB882 is another survivor from that first batch. She joined 428 'Ghost' Squadron RCAF in March 1945 as 'NA-R' and flew on six operational sorties over Germany. On 2 June, she was flown back to Canada by her RCAF crew and went into storage in Alberta. In 1952 she was ferried to A V Roe (Canada) for a major overhaul and modification to Mark 10P – photographic – configuration. The most noticeable alteration was the addition of a 40-inch extension to the nose section. Like KB839, she went into service with 408 Squadron and in the late 1940s and 1950s was used to photograph most of the Canadian High Arctic.

Like FM213, she was retired to Dunnville. Then in 1964 the aircraft was bought by the City of Edmundston, New Brunswick, and is on display outside the Municipal Airport.

The other surviving Lancasters were used as training aircraft or were constructed too late to see service in World War II.

NX611 'Just Jane' – a Mark VII – was part of the third production batch of 150 aircraft built by Austin at Longbridge. Serial numbers in this batch included NX611–NX648, NX661–NX703, NX715–NX758 and NX770–NX794. There are four survivors from the batch. Deliveries started in April 1945 and ended in September 1945 at an average of six a week.

Above: 'Jane' appeared in a comic strip in the Daily Mirror throughout World War II. She had trouble keeping her clothes on and was seen to boost the morale of the armed forces. She was adopted as a mascot by the crew of NX611, a Lancaster Mark VII.

NX611 was one of 22 Lancasters sold to the Aeronavale – the French naval air force – and was delivered in June 1952. Retired in the 1960s, she was donated to the Historic Aircraft Museum in Sydney, Australia. Later, she was flown back to Britain. At one stage the aircraft was kept at Blackpool, then took over from R5868 as gate guardian at RAF Scampton. She is now on display at the Lincolnshire Aviation Heritage Centre at the former RAF East Kirkby. Although she is not airworthy, she is frequently taxied at high speed along a length of the wartime runway.

NX622 – another Mark VII – came from the same batch as NX611 and served with the Aeronavale. In 1962, she was donated to the RAAF Association. After restoration work, she went on display at the RAAF Association Museum in Bull Creek, Western Australia.

Left: *East Kirby not only has the Lancaster, it is also the only airfield in England recreated to its original design and sited on an original World War II airfield. It is seen as a memorial to Bomber Command but is also a tribute to Christopher Whitton Panton, brother of the owners, who perished in a Lancaster during the war.*

Below: *Displayed at the Museum of Transport and Technology (MOTAT) in Auckland, New Zealand, Lancaster NX665 was built in 1945, but was too late to see action in World War II. After being in storage she was sent to the French Naval Air Arm in 1952 and saw service in the South Pacific before her last flight to MOTAT for restoration in 1964.*

NX664 and NX665 were also from the same batch as NX611 and NX622 and served with the Aeronavale. NX664 was retired after making a heavy landing at Wallis Island in French Polynesia. In 1984, she was returned to Le Bourget to be restored at Saint-Mande.

In the 1960s, Aeronavale donated NX665 to the Museum of Transport and Technology in Western Springs in Auckland, New Zealand. The airframe was missing the mid-upper turret. It had been built with the mountings for a Martin 250CE, but an earlier FN50 was retrofitted in the late 1980s. This required modifications to the aircraft's structure as the turret mounts had to be moved rearwards. She is also equipped with H2S radar.

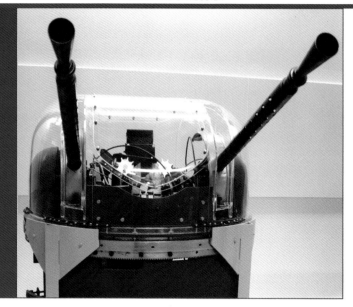

Left: There are many different Lancaster parts that have survived the traumas of World War II, and there are hundreds of museums around the world that display not only whole Lancasters but also their engines, cockpits and many other varied parts of the aircraft. Seen here is a Martin mid-upper turret, whilst RAF Duxford in England also houses a Lancaster which was built in Canada in 1944 and served with 428 Squadron (Royal Canadian Air Force) in England (right and below).

KB889 was from the same batch as KB839 and KB882. She was delivered to Britain in March 1945 and assigned to 428 Squadron, but she returned to Canada on 4 June without seeing any service. She was then converted for maritime reconnaissance with 408 Squadron. Retired in 1965, she was on display in Ontario before being sold to collector Doug Arnold in 1984 and returned to Britain. She was put on the UK register as G-LANC, but was never flown. In 1986, she was sold to the Imperial War Museum and, over the next eight years, was restored as a static display bearing the identification code 'NA-I'. Since 1994, she has been on display at the air museum at Duxford.

The Imperial War Museum also have on display the cockpit section of a Mark I Lancaster, serial number DV372. It was part of the third production batch of 200 aircraft built by Metropolitan-Vickers. Of this order 91 aircraft were completed as Mark Is. The rest were completed as Mark IIIs. Delivery started May 1943 and finished in November 1943. By then, production had risen to eight planes a week. Sadly, DV372's cockpit is all that remains of that batch.

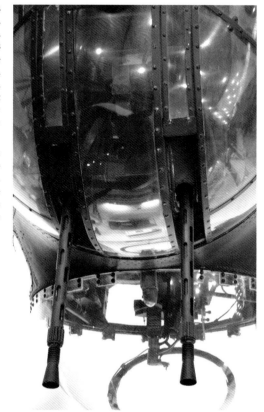

ve & Left: *Lancaster Mk X, FM136 is housed in the*
Space Museum, Calgary, Canada. It was one of the
to be built at the Victory Aircraft Works in Malton,
rio, Canada, and was never issued to an active
dron. It is owned by the City of Calgary.

Also from the first Canadian production batch, KB944 was also flown to Britain in March. She was assigned to 425 Squadron as 'KW-K', then returned to Canada on 15 June to go into storage. She served briefly with 404 'Buffalo' Maritime Patrol Squadron at Greenwood, Nova Scotia, in 1952. In 1964 the RCAF refurbished this aircraft for the Armed Force's historical aircraft collection. It is now on public display at the National Aviation Museum in Ottawa.

KB976 was only delivered to Britain in May 1945 and consequently saw no action, though she was assigned to 405 Squadron as 'LQ-K'. Returning to Canada on 17 June 1945, she was converted for aerial reconnaissance with 408 Squadron. Retired in 1964, she was the last RCAF Mark to fly, making her final flight at the Calgary International Air Show on 4 July 1964. The pilot on that flight, Flight Lieutenant Lynn Garrison, bought KB976 for the Air Museum of Canada, which he had opened that April. In 1974, she was sold to the Strathallan Collection in Scotland and flown back across the Atlantic. She was on static display there until 1987, when she was bought by collector Charles Church and moved to Woodford for restoration to airworthy condition. However, the airframe was damaged when a hangar collapsed. The rebuild was abandoned and the aircraft was sold to Doug Arnold. Then, in 1992, she was bought by American collector Kermit Weeks in 1992 who took her to his Fantasy of Flight museum in Florida for restoration.

Part of two more planes from that first batch of Mark Xs survive. KB941 was delivered to 420 Squadron as 'PT-U' in April 1945. She returned to Canada on 14 June and remained with the RCAF at Penhold, Alberta until the 1960s. The centre section survives in private hands.

KB994 was delivered to 408 Squadron as 'EQ-K' in June 1945, after the war in Europe was over. She returned to Canada on 16 June and served with the RCAF at Penhold, Alberta until the 1960s. She was then acquired by 408 Squadron in Edmonton, Alberta. Sold on to Charles Church, she was shipped to England for the air museum at North Weald Airfield in Essex. However, there are rumours that the remains have been sold to a collector in America.

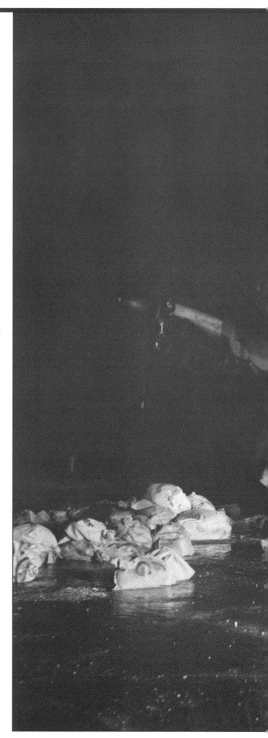

Right: Operation Manna distributed food and supplies to the Dutch populace. Here, ground crew prepare to load sacks of food into the bomb bay of an Avro Lancaster of 514 Squadron at Waterbeach, Cambridgeshire.

As well as Canada's only airworthy Lancaster FM213, other planes survived from that second batch from Victory Aircraft Ltd. FM104 was flown to England in January 1945, stored at 32 Maintenance Unit awaiting assignment to a squadron, then returned to Canada in June 1945 where she was modified for maritime reconnaissance and assigned to No 10 Rescue Unit. In 1964, the Lancaster was donated to the City of Toronto and placed on a plinth in Lakeshore Drive. After sitting outside for 36 years, she was taken down and loaned to the Toronto Aerospace Museum for restoration in static display condition. Using spare parts from the remainder of FM118, the restoration should be complete in 2015, when she will go on display.

FM118 was also from that second batch from Victory Aircraft Ltd. She was flown to England in April 1945 and, like FM104, she was stored at 32 Maintenance Unit awaiting assignment to a squadron. But the end of the war came and she was returned to Canada in June 1945. Most of her fuselage is in storage at the Nanton Lancaster Society Air Museum in Alberta. Other surviving pieces are in storage at the British Commonwealth Air Training Plan Museum in Brandon, Manitoba.

Another of that second batch, FM136, was flown to England in May 1945, stored at 32 Maintenance Unit, then returned to Canada in August 1945. Converted for maritime reconnaissance, she joined 404 'Buffalo' Maritime Patrol Squadron at Greenwood, Nova Scotia, as RX-136. She was later transferred to 407 'Demon' Maritime Patrol Squadron at Comox, British Columbia where she remained in service until April 1961. Then she was bought by Lynn Garrison, who later bought KB976. He created the Lancaster Memorial Fund to get the aircraft displayed on a plinth at McCall Field, Calgary, as a memorial to those who trained under the British Commonwealth Air Training Plan. In 1992, she moved to the Aerospace Museum of Calgary, where a new shelter was built for the plane in 2007.

FM159 arrived in Europe after the war there was over, and never saw combat. After returning to Canada and being placed in storage, she was converted for maritime reconnaissance. She served from 1953 to 1955 with the 103 Search and Rescue Unit in Greenwood, Nova Scotia, before being transferred to 407 Squadron at Comox, British Columbia, to serve as a maritime and ice patrol aircraft. She was retired from service by the RCAF in 1959. In 1960 she was bought and is currently on display at the Nanton Lancaster Society Air Museum, one of only two surviving Lancasters to offer guided tours of the interior.

In 1991, the Nanton Lancaster Society dedicated Lancaster FM159 to Ian Bazalgette VC of 635 Squadron. FM159 now carries the markings of his aircraft F2-T. In 2005 she was rolled out of the hangar for her first engine run-up in over 30 years. After a couple of minor problems were sorted out, her number three engine coughed into life with the usual puff of smoke.

FM212 – 'Bad Penny' – did not even get to fly the Atlantic. She was retained in Canada and used on a photographic survey by 413 Photo Squadron RCAF in 1947 before being transferred to 408 Squadron at Rockcliffe, Ottawa, in 1949. There her tasks included photo-mapping, reconnaissance, search and rescue, ice patrols, aircrew training and navigation exercises. She had logged 8,069.5 hours by the time she was retired from service by the RCAF in 1962 and placed in storage. The City of Windsor, Ontario, bought the aircraft and mounted it on a plinth in Jackson Park in 1965 as a memorial to the 400 airmen from the area who had lost their lives in World War II. Weather and poor maintenance damaged the fabric of the plane and she was replaced by replicas of a Spitfire and a Hurricane on 26 May 2005. The Canadian Historical Aircraft Association then began a comprehensive restoration.

On 29 April 2007 – the 62nd anniversary of Operation Manna when Lancasters dropped food to the Dutch in the last days of the war – FM212 was removed from storage in Jackson Park and towed to the Sears parking lot of Devonshire Mall where she went on display for two weeks. Then she was towed to Windsor Airport where the restoration continues.

Sadly, FM221, another Mark X retained in Canada, crashed on 23 September 1950, at Resolute Bay in the North West Territories of Canada, where the wreckage can still be seen.

Below: *The original 'Phantom of the Ruhr', Lancaster EE139, with the emblem quite clearly seen. This aircraft flew with 100 Squadron and then with 550 Squadron during World War II. The Battle of Britain Memorial Flight (BBMF) Lancaster commemorates the original Lancaster and wears the phantom emblem (bottom right), even though it is not the actual aircraft. Note also the 'ice cream cones' beside the phantom emblem, depicting Italian campaigns.*

The 'Phantom of the Ruhr'

Lancaster EE139 was built by A V Roe Ltd at their Newton Heath works in Manchester. Part of an order for 620 aircraft, she was built as a Mark III aircraft powered by Packard Merlin 28 engines. She was delivered to 100 Squadron RAF Grimsby at the end of May 1943.

Sergeant Ron Clark and his crew arrived at Grimsby at the same time as EE139 and flew her for the first time on 2 June 1943. After successfully completing seven training flights, EE139 was assigned to the bombing of the Ruhr that had then been going on for four months. On 11 June they joined 783 heavy bombers in an attack on the heavily defended city of Düsseldorf. EE139 found herself flying 21,000 feet over the 'Valley of Hell' – a solid wall of flak between Cologne and Düsseldorf. She bombed factories and rail yards, and returned miraculously unscathed to Grimsby. That night the squadron lost 2 Lancasters and 13 men; one man survived the shoot-down to become a prisoner of war. By then only two crews survived from those that had reformed 100 Squadron at Grimsby in December 1942. That month alone, nine crews were lost, one-third of the squadron's strength.

The plane took its name from the film *Phantom of the Opera* that was showing at that time. The motif – a ghoulish hooded skeleton figure throwing bombs out of the night sky – was designed by the flight engineer, Harold 'Ben' Bennett. Initially code named FZ-A, depicting 'C' Flight of 100 Squadron, she became HW-R for Roger in July 1943.

Sergeant Clark piloted the 'Phantom' on 42 sorties, logging over 165 hours in the plane. Of these, 147 were on night operations. He would captain the aircraft on 25 of the 33 operations EE139 would undertake with 100 Squadron. Of those 33 operations, 3 were aborted, so when EE139 left 100 Squadron in November 1943, she had 30 'ops' painted in two rows on her side. Operational sorties were represented by yellow bombs with a red bomb signifying an attack on Berlin. Operations to Italy were recorded with an ice cream cone. Sergeant Clark and his crew were responsible for two of the four cones on EE139, including an 11-hour flight to Turin. He also flew her to Berlin three times and four times to Hamburg in what became known as the 'Battle of Hamburg' of July 1943. There were other flights to Cologne, Essen and Nuremberg.

On 17 August 1943 the 'Phantom' took part in the Peenemunde raid on the secret V-2 rocket research establishment on the Baltic. Having dropped their 1,000lb bombs from 8,000 feet, Clark made use of the perfect moonlight conditions, descending to tree-top height to allow his gunners to shoot up targets of opportunity.

On the night of 22 September, the 'Phantom' was beginning its bomb run on Mannheim at 21,000 feet when she was caught in a searchlight. Clark threw the plane into a dive, but the searchlights stayed on her. The aircraft was hit by flak. A shell came in through the bomb doors and went out through the topside of the fuselage without exploding. However, it severed the cable controlling the starboard aileron, sending the plane out of control. Clark and flight engineer 'Ben' Bennett fought to regain at 13,000 feet, but the searchlights were on her. A night fighter attacked from the rear, damaging the port wing flap. Another shell hit the starboard tailplane.

Clark could see streams of tracer in front of him, and threw the plane into another dive. Shaking the fighter, he recovered the aircraft again at only 4,000 feet. Clearing the target area they jettisoned their bombs, but the plane was vibrating violently with the port wing and the tailplane flapping up and down. Armed with a pair of pliers, Bennett cut the control wires to the starboard aileron trim tab which stopped the vibration. Then with no flaps and only partial aileron control, Clark nursed the crippled bomber home. Clark and Bennett were awarded the Distinguished Flying Cross and Distinguished Flying Medal respectively.

While the 'Phantom' was being repaired, the tail fin from a 30lb incendiary bomb was found in the air intake of one of the engines, showing that the aircraft had been hit by bombs dropped from above. There was also severe damage to the tail and rudder and there were at least 300 shrapnel holes in the aircraft.

EE139 flew four more operations with 100 Squadron before being transferred to the newly formed 550 Squadron on 25 November 1943. After more trips to the Ruhr, Flight Sergeant Bouchard and his crew took EE139 on five raids on Berlin before the end of the year. She visited Berlin four more times during January 1944, when 550 Squadron moved to North Killingholme, EE139's home for the rest of the war.

On 5 September 1944, she became the first of 550 Squadron's planes to clock up 100 missions with a daylight raid on Le Havre. The pilot was Flying Officer Hutcheson, and his crew were: flight engineer Sergeant Wright, navigator Sergeant Smith, bomb aimer Flight Sergeant Francis of the RAAF, wireless operator Warrant Officer Smith of the RAAF, dorsal gunner Sergeant Hodgson and rear gunner Sergeant Tosh. Between 22 June 1944 and 23 September 1944, this crew flew 30 missions on board the 'Phantom', completing a full operational tour on one aircraft.

On her 102nd operation, a raid on Frankfurt, EE139 again suffered flak damage and was attacked three times by a Messerschmitt Me109. Somehow she survived. Two missions later, the 'Phantom' was landing in the wet at North Killingholme after returning from Stuttgart, when she aquaplaned the entire length of the runway, coming to a stand on her nose in a field. Still, EE139 was patched up and went on to make a further 17 trips.

On 21 November 1944, after a night raid on the Aschaffenburg railway marshalling yards, the pilot became alarmed by the handling of the aircraft. He concluded that the airframe was twisted and the aircraft was retired from operations.

EE139 had been on 121 missions and completed 830 hours of operational flying. Three times she had been damaged beyond capacity of the unit to repair, but still returned to the air. She was just 18 months old when she was retired. EE139 was then used as a trainer. Despite eventually becoming 550 Squadron's longest serving Lancaster, the 'Phantom' was unceremoniously scrapped in February 1946.

Below: Reconnaissance photo, taken over Le Havre, France after daylight raids by aircraft of Bomber Command on 5, 6 and 8 September 1944. A large area of devastation can be seen in the city centre west of the Bassin de Commerce, over which smoke from burning buildings is drifting. Further attacks on and around Le Havre were carried out on the three following days in an effort to reduce the German garrison still holding out in the city.

Andrew Mynarski VC

Warrant Officer Andrew Mynarski was a mid-upper gunner in 419 'Moose' Squadron, flying out of RAF Middleton St George in Yorkshire. In early June 1944, his crew was given the Lancaster Mark X bomber, KB726, coded 'VR-A' – call sign A for Able.

On 12 June 1944, Mynarski was aboard VR-A which was making a raid on northern France. After meeting flak over the coastline, and being briefly targeted or 'coned' by searchlights, the Lancaster was attacked by a Ju-88 night fighter over Cambrai. Cannon fire knocked out both port engines and hit the centre fuselage, engulfing the plane in fire. The captain, Flight Officer Art de Breyne, ordered the crew to bail out. When Mynarski reached the rear escape door, he saw through the flames that his friend, the tail gunner Pilot Officer Pat Brophy, was trapped. His turret was jammed part way through its rotation to the escape position.

Mynarski made his way through the inferno to help Brophy. He tried using a fire axe to pry the doors open, finally resorting to beating at the turret with his hands. By this time his clothing and parachute were on fire and Brophy waved him away. Mynarski crawled back through the fire to the rear door. He saluted and said, "Good night, sir." Then he jumped.

The shroud lines on his parachute were burnt and he descended rapidly. He landed heavily with his clothes on fire. He was still alive when a French farmer reached him, but died of severe burns in a German field hospital shortly after.

The other five crew members escaped through the front hatch and survived. Pat Brophy was still trapped in the bomber when it hit the ground. He survived the crash. When the bomb load detonated, he was thrown, alive, from the tail turret. Rescued by the French Resistance, he fought alongside them behind enemy lines, making it back to London in September 1944 where he learned of Mynarski's death.

The navigator Robert Bodie, radio operator James Kelly and pilot Art de Breyne were hidden by the French and returned to England shortly after the crash. Flight engineer Roy Vigars and the wounded bomb aimer Jack Friday were captured by the Germans and interned until they could be liberated by American troops.

On 11 October 1946, Andrew Mynarski was posthumously awarded a Victoria Cross and promoted to the rank of Pilot Officer.

Ian Bazalgette VC

On 4 August 1944, Squadron Leader Ian Bazalgette was master bomber of a Pathfinder squadron detailed to mark an important target at Trossy St Maximin for the main bomber force. Nearing the target, his Lancaster came under heavy anti-aircraft fire. Both starboard engines were put out of action and serious fires broke out in the fuselage and the starboard main-plane. The bomb aimer was badly wounded.

As the deputy master bomber had already been shot down, Bazalgette knew that the success of the attack depended on him. Despite the fact that his plane was on fire, he pressed on to the target, marking and bombing it accurately. The attack was successful.

After he had dropped his bombs, Bazalgette's Lancaster went into a steep dive. After a struggle he regained control. But the port inner engine then failed and the whole of the starboard of the plane was a mass of flames. Bazalgette ordered the crew to bail out. He remained at the controls in an attempt to land the crippled aircraft and save the lives of the wounded bomb aimer and the mid-upper gunner who had been overcome by fumes.

From his parachute, wireless operator Chuck Godfrey watched as the blazing bomber approached the tiny French village of Senates. Somehow Bazalgette managed to turn the bomber away from the houses. He landed the Lancaster in a field, but the fuel exploded in a huge fireball, killing all three on board.

Acknowledgements

The Author and Publisher would like to thank the following people and organizations for their contribution to this book:

The quote from the speech made by Winston Churchill is reproduced with permission of Curtis Brown Ltd, London, on behalf of The Estate of Winston Churchill.

Copyright © Winston S Churchill.

Imperial War Museum, London, England.

The AVRO Heritage Centre, Stockport, Cheshire, England.

Spink (medals dpt.), London, England.

©Annette Koolsbergen/Canadian Warplane Heritage Museum, 0Canada – Page 232–3.

Greenwood Military Aviation Museum, Nova Scotia, Canada/ Picture courtesy of Major Bert Campbell, RCAF/CAF retired – Page 237.

Museum of Transport and Technology (MOTAT), Auckland, New Zealand – Page 241.

Aero Space Museum Association of Calgary, Calgary, Canada – Page 244–5.

Battle of Britain Memorial Flight, Lincolnshire, England.

RAF Museum, Hendon, London, England.

Imperial War Museum, Duxford, England.

RAF Scampton, Lincoln, England.

Lincolnshire Aviation Heritage Museum, East Kirkby, Lincoln, England.

Bundesarchive, Koblenz, Germany.

US Library of Congress, Washington DC, USA.

US National Archives, Washington DC, USA.

Air Team Images – www.AirTeamImages.com

Rolls-Royce Heritage Trust.

Rolls-Royce Plc.

ED Archives, Edgmond, Newport, England.

Cody Images, Beith, Scotland.

Copyright@EADS – Page 122 (top).

Front Cover – Avro 683 Lancaster – © Skyscan/Corbis.